"十二五"职业教育国家规划教材
经全国职业教育教材审定委员会审定

A New English Course for Business Studies
—Reading Skills 1

新商务英语阅读教程 1

总 主 编：杨亚军 周瑞杰 谢职安
主   编：程 可
副 主 编：马亚星 孟庆丰
编   著：揣维维 许婉亭

清华大学出版社
北 京

内容简介

"新商务英语教程"系列教材采用话题、语言技能和任务紧密结合的编写原则,以话题为核心,语言技能为主线,精心设计的任务型活动贯穿每个教学单元。本书为《新商务英语阅读教程1》,全书共8个单元,每单元由 Learning Objectives,Lead-in,Embracing English, Extending Your English 和 Self-evaluation 5 个模块构成,在扩大阅读量的同时对英语阅读基本技能进行训练。

本教材可供高职高专院校商务英语专业和应用英语专业的外贸和涉外文秘方向一年级学生使用。

本书封面贴有清华大学出版社防伪标签,无标签者不得销售。
版权所有,侵权必究。举报: 010-62782989,beiqinquan@tup.tsinghua.edu.cn。

图书在版编目(CIP)数据

新商务英语阅读教程. 1 / 程可主编. —北京: 清华大学出版社,2015(2023.7重印)
新商务英语教程
ISBN 978-7-302-37098-7

I. ①新… II. ①程… III. ①商务-英语-阅读教学-教材 IV. ① H319.4

中国版本图书馆 CIP 数据核字(2014)第 146040 号

责任编辑:赵洛育
装帧设计:张 宇
责任校对:赵丽杰
责任印制:刘海龙

出版发行:清华大学出版社
网　　址:http://www.tup.com.cn,http://www.wqbook.com
地　　址:北京清华大学学研大厦 A 座　　邮　编:100084
社 总 机:010-83470000　　邮　购:010-62786544
投稿与读者服务:010-62776969,c-service@tup.tsinghua.edu.cn
质 量 反 馈:010-62772015,zhiliang@tup.tsinghua.edu.cn

印 装 者:三河市龙大印装有限公司
经　　销:全国新华书店
开　　本:185mm×260mm　　印 张:9　　字　数:224 千字
版　　次:2015 年 5 月第 1 版　　印　次:2023 年 7 月第 6 次印刷
定　　价:39.80 元

产品编号:053547-01

"新商务英语教程"系列教材
丛书编委会

主　任：牛　健（北京信息科技大学）

　　　　丁　岭（清华大学出版社）

副主任：杨亚军（北京联合大学）

编　委：（以姓氏笔画排序）

　　　　王君华（河南经贸职业学院）

　　　　邹　枚（特约编辑）

　　　　周瑞杰（黑龙江建筑职业技术学院）

　　　　彭　丽（重庆工商职业学院）

　　　　谢职安（北京联合大学）

　　　　戴明元（四川建筑职业技术学院）

前言
PREFACE

　　《新商务英语阅读教程》是"新商务英语教程"系列教材的主干教材之一。编写此套教材旨在为高职高专商务英语专业及应用英语专业学生提供适合学生的英语水平及阅读能力、有效提升他们的专业与职业素养的专业基础课教材,为培养应用型、技能型、职业型国际商务贸易人才服务。

　　《新商务英语阅读教程》共4个分册。全套教材本着"围绕商务相关主题学习知识和复现知识"的原则,以话题为核心,以阅读学习和技巧训练为主线,采用英语语言知识和商务知识有机结合的编写方式,注重语言知识和商务知识紧密衔接,非常适合高职高专英语专业学生的学习能力和水平。本套教材选文题材广泛、内容丰富,涵盖金融、财经、管理、外贸、电子商务等诸多商务领域,使学生既能提高英语阅读理解能力,又能系统地掌握商务英语的基本词汇及其表达方式。若配合本系列教材中的《新商务英语综合教程》和《新商务英语听说教程》各分册使用,则能帮助学生更系统地掌握商务英语的基本词汇及其表达方式,全面地获得有关商务的基本知识。

　　本教材为《新商务英语阅读教程1》,分为8个单元。每单元设计为4个部分,Section A 以与本单元主题相关的导入学习为主要内容,这部分的构建注重图文并茂,以调动学生的视觉,从各方面投入本单元的学习;同时能让师生"先入为主"地了解每单元的教学主题,使师生双方都处于主动地位。Section B 由课文 Text A 和 Text B 及相应练习组成,其中 Text A 作为主课文使用,目的是有针对性地培养商务英语专业学生的综合阅读能力,通过练习注重词汇的多层次使用和词汇学习策略(记忆、扩展)的介绍,同时兼顾已学的语言知识、商务知识及阅读技能的复现。Text B 是快速阅读训练(Fast Reading)的课文,设计的思路是培养学生在有限的时间内快速、准确地获取主要信息的能力,此部分可在课堂规定的时间内完成。课文后的练习设计关注语篇呈现,适当拓展,即引导学生学会学习相关知识,而非只关注结果。Section C 专门针对某项阅读技能来指导和训练学生,并以此为原则来选择文章和设计练习,这部分由阅读技巧讲解、技能训练短文及相应的练习组成,其设计特别强调阅读技巧的讲解与运用的体现。以上3个部分练习的设计在关注学生语言知识和阅读技能训练的同时,注重培养学生的学习策略、情感和文化等素养。每单元的 Section C 是专门设计的 Self-evaluation,思路是鼓励学生不断反思自己的学习过程,肯定进步,找出问题,不断优化学习方式。学生的评价结果也有利于教师及时发现教学中存在的问题,调整教学内容和教学方法。

　　为了解决学生词汇量少、阅读量小和阅读速度慢的难题,每单元的课文之后还附有词汇表,且有注音,词汇表使用双语,让学生通过英语学英语;课文后还对一些难词难句加了注解,并将平时提及较少的人名、地名列在注释中,有些还加注了必要的商务背景知识,对引导学生扩大知识面有一定启迪和裨益。

本教材可供高等职业学校、高等专科学校以及成人高等学校商务英语专业的学生使用，亦可用作爱好英语的非商务英语专业学生的自学课本。各学校在使用本教材时可根据学生英语及商务知识的基础灵活掌握。

本教材在编写过程中参阅了大量国内外英语教材及文献，同时听取了许多专家的宝贵意见和建议，北京联合大学的英籍专家Colin James Osland对全书进行了文字审定，在此一并表示谢忱。

由于时间仓促，水平有限，错误和疏漏之处在所难免，敬请读者批评指正。

编　者

2014 年 7 月

目录
CONTENTS

Unit 1 **Introduction** 1
    Learning Objectives 1
        Section A   Lead-in 2
        Section B   Embracing English 2
            Text A   Introducing Yourself Makes an Impact! 2
            Text B   I'd Like for You to Meet Mr. Raynes 8
        Section C   Extending Your English 12
            I. Approaching the reading skill: understanding main points and supporting details
（理解文章主旨要义）... 12
            II. Applying the reading skill: Outdated? —Only Introduce Men to Women 14
        Section D   Self-evaluation 16

Unit 2 **Job Interview** 17
    Learning Objectives 17
        Section A   Lead-in 18
        Section B   Embracing English 18
            Text A   Sharing My Job Interview Experience 18
            Text B   Some Common Types of Job Interviews 23
        Section C   Extending Your English 27
            I. Approaching the reading skill: understanding the text organization（理解文章结构）... 27
            II. Applying the reading skill: How to Prepare for a Job Interview 28
        Section D   Self-evaluation 30

Unit 3 **A New Job** 31
    Learning Objectives 31
        Section A   Lead-in 32
        Section B   Embracing English 32
            Text A   On Your First Day at a New Job 32
            Text B   The Mistakes You Can Make When You Start a New Job 37
        Section C   Extending Your English 41

I. Approaching the reading skill: understanding stated information（理解明确表达的信息）1 41

II. Applying the reading skill: Remember Your Very First Day of Work? 42

Section D　Self-evaluation 44

Unit 4　On-the-Job Training 45

Learning Objectives 45

Section A　Lead-in 46

Section B　Embracing English 46

Text A　Why Is Workplace Training Important? 46

Text B　Employee Coaching: When to Step In 52

Section C　Extending Your English 56

I. Approaching the reading skill: understanding stated information（理解明确表达的信息）2 56

II. Applying the reading skill: On-the-job Training 57

Section D　Self-evaluation 60

Unit 5　Phone Calls 61

Learning Objectives 61

Section A　Lead-in 62

Section B　Embracing English 62

Text A　Time Management Tips for Outgoing Telephone Calls 62

Text B　Time Management Tips for Inbound Phone Calls 67

Section C　Extending Your English 71

I. Approaching the reading skill: guessing unknown words（猜测生词词义）1 71

II. Applying the reading skill: How to Make a Good Impression on the Phone 72

Section D　Self-evaluation 74

Unit 6　Agenda 75

Learning Objectives 75

Section A　Lead-in 76

Section B　Embracing English 76

Text A　How to Structure an Agenda 76

Text B　How to Organize a Web Conference Agenda 81

Section C　Extending Your English 85

  I. Approaching the reading skill: guessing unknown words（猜测生词词义）2 85

  II. Applying the reading skill: The Advantages of an Agenda 86

 Section D Self-evaluation 88

Unit 7 Meetings 89

 Learning Objectives 89

 Section A Lead-in 90

 Section B Embracing English 90

  Text A About Business Meetings 90

  Text B Increase Attendance for Business Meetings 95

 Section C Extending Your English 99

  I. Approaching the reading skill: scanning to locate specifically required information

  （查读）1 99

  II. Applying the reading skill: Make Business Meetings Fun 100

 Section D Self-evaluation 102

Unit 8 Business Travel 103

 Learning Objectives 103

 Section A Lead-in 104

 Section B Embracing English 104

  Text A How to Make Travel Arrangements & Itinerary 104

  Text B Travel Tips for Elite Treatment 109

 Section C Extending Your English 113

  I. Approaching the reading skill: scanning to locate specifically required information

  （查读）2 113

  II. Applying the reading skill: Travel Arrangements 114

 Section D Self-evaluation 116

New Words and Expressions 117

Unit 1

Introduction

Learning Objectives

In this unit, you will learn

- to understand the importance of making proper introductions;
- to get basic information about the self-introduction;
- to master the new words and expressions related to making introductions;
- to apply the reading skill—understanding main points and supporting details.

Section A / Lead-in

I. Can you name the following ways of greeting?

Directions: Match the words or expressions in the box with the pictures.

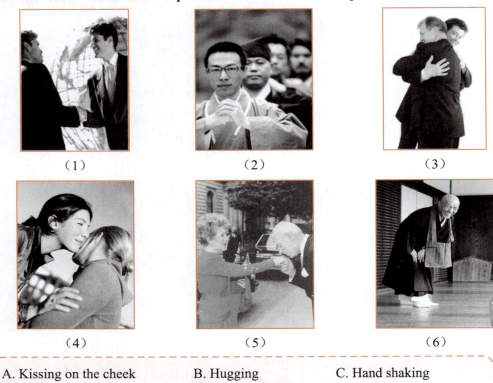

(1) (2) (3) (4) (5) (6)

```
A. Kissing on the cheek      B. Hugging        C. Hand shaking
D. Hand kissing              E. Bowing         F. Holding fist salute
```

II. Describe the above pictures.

Directions: Work in pairs to describe the above greeting ways you know best.

Section B / Embracing English

Text A

Pre-reading Task: Answer the following questions before reading the text.

1. Why do we have to make a self-introduction?

2. What can we say for making a self-introduction to other people?

3. What do you think is a successful self-introduction?

Introducing Yourself Makes an Impact!

Here it is, the all-important moment your **palms** have been **sweating** about.[1] Everyone wants to make a good first **impression**, and a winning self-introduction is a good way to start. It may be at school, at church, in the workplace or at a team building game. We all know a great deal about ourselves! So sell yourself and make a good impression. The **stage** is all yours—**insight** into you—for a great impact and impression![2]

Remember the purpose for introducing yourself. Whether you are making a **personal** introduction or being introduced for the purpose of making a **contact**, your first impression is **critical** to your **success** at leaving a good impression upon a new person. Always remember that the introduction's **sole** purpose is to let all those **involved** and being introduced know who is who.[3] Sounds simple but remember that everyone involved is forming opinions **based on** your appearance, speech, clothing, words and **manners**. First impressions can either make or break you.

Get fully prepared for introducing yourself. You only have a few minutes, so you cannot tell your **audience** everything about yourself. So, choose 3 or 4 main areas of your life and **elaborate** with a few key ideas on them. **Depending on** your age and the **composition** of your audience, you may select a few of the following topics to include for further discussion: your education and **qualifications**; your work experience; your family and background; your future **ambitions** and dreams; favorite hobbies; or something that the audience may find surprising to learn about you.

Take **practical** steps for introducing yourself. Self-introduction is also the key to go success, because you are starting from a **baseline** position where they have no experience of who you are or what you are like.[4] Some basic steps may work to **ensure** great introductions and consequently great first impressions.

Stand up or **lean** down. If you start introducing yourself as you're getting up out of your chair, it's **guaranteed** that people will miss some of what you're saying. You should try to put yourself **on equal ground**. This is respectful but it also enables you to meet the person **eye to eye**.

Be **confident**. As you start you should always show confidence. If you are not confident about yourself, make the necessary changes in order to be able to give yourself this **edge**. **In addition**, be prepared and confident in your story. While you certainly do not want to give the appearance as **boastful** or prideful, people need to know that you believe in what you are saying, and your attitude will go a long way toward assuring them that you do.

"Smile and shake and smile and shake". Everyone will agree that this is perfect advice. We were meeting new people so what do you do? When you meet someone new you smile, showing yourself to be friendly, and offer a firm handshake which is a most popular **gesture** of friendship.

Pay careful attention to your speech. Remember your goal is not only to make someone's **acquaintance** but also to have the chance to share your story and thinking. Communication involves listening, understanding and speaking. Involve yourself in all three of these activities during your speech. Be attentive and just be careful not to **embarrass** or upset your audience.

Manners matter learning to **interact** with grace and **etiquette** is very important for your success.

Your personality and style is one of the key things you have either going for or against you. Remember it has been rightly said that no matter what you are doing or where you are going, you are always the **constant**.⁵

Share a **quote** with your audience. Find a quote that is significant and meaningful to your life. Memorize it and conclude your **icebreaker** speech with a powerful quote that leaves the audience with insight into YOU!

There you go, easy peasy!⁶

(664 words)

New Words and Expressions

impact /ˈɪmpækt/	n.	powerful effect that something, especially something new, has on a situation or person 影响；作用
palm /pɑːm/	n.	the inside part of your hand from your wrist to the base of your fingers 手掌
sweat /swet/	v.	to pass sweat through the skin because you are hot, ill, or frightened 出汗
impression /ɪmˈpreʃn/	n.	an idea or opinion of what something or someone is like 印象
stage /steɪdʒ/	n.	the area in a theatre that is often raised above ground level and on which actors or entertainers perform 舞台
insight /ˈɪnsaɪt/	n.	a clear, deep, and sometimes sudden understanding of a complicated problem or situation 洞察力，眼光
personal /ˈpɜːsənl/	adj.	relating or belonging to a single or particular person rather than to a group or an organization 个人的
contact /ˈkɒntækt/	n.	communication with someone, especially by speaking or writing to them regularly 交往；联系，联络
critical /ˈkrɪtɪkəl/	adj.	of the greatest importance to the way things might happen 紧要的，关键性的；危急的
success /səkˈses/	n.	the achieving of the results wanted or hoped for 成功
sole /səʊl/	n.	being one only; single 单独的；唯一的
involve /ɪnˈvɒlv/	v.	to include someone or something in something, or to make them take part in or feel part of it 使卷入，连累；牵涉
manner /ˈmænər/	n.	polite ways of treating other people and behaving in public （常用复数）礼貌；规矩
audience /ˈɔːdiəns/	n.	the group of people together in one place to watch or listen to a play, film, someone speaking, etc. 听众，观众
elaborate /ɪˈlæbəreɪt/	v.	to add more information to or explain something that you have said 详细制定；详尽阐述
composition /ˌkɒmpəˈzɪʃn/	n.	the parts, substances, etc. that something is made of 构成；构图；成分

qualification /ˌkwɒlɪfɪˈkeɪʃən/	n.		an ability, characteristic, or experience that makes you suitable for a particular job or activity 资格，职权；能力
ambition /æmˈbɪʃən/	n.		a strong wish to achieve something 雄心，抱负
practical /ˈpræktɪkəl/	adj.		relating to experience, real situations, or actions rather than ideas or imagination 实际的；实用的
baseline /ˈbeɪslaɪn/	n.		a line or measurement that is used as a starting point when comparing facts（用于比较的）基础，起点
ensure /ɪnˈʃʊə/	v.		to make something certain to happen 保证；担保
lean /liːn/	v.		to (cause to) slope in one direction, or to move the top part of the body in a particular direction（使）倾斜，屈身
guarantee /ˌɡærənˈtiː/	v.		to make something certain to happen 保障；保证……免受损失
confident /ˈkɒnfɪdənt/	adj.		the quality of being certain of your abilities or of having trust in people, plans, or the future 自信的
edge /edʒ/	n.		an advantage over other people 优势
boastful /ˈbəʊstfəl/	adj.		praising yourself and what you have done 自夸的；爱自夸的
gesture /ˈdʒestʃə/	n.		a movement of the hands, arms, or head, etc. to express an idea or feeling 姿势；手势
acquaintance /əˈkweɪntəns/	n.		a person that you have met but do not know well 相识的人，熟人
embarrass /ɪmˈbærəs/	v.		to cause someone to feel nervous, worried, or uncomfortable 使窘迫；使不好意思，使局促不安
interact /ˌɪntərˈækt/	v.		to communicate with or react to 互动
etiquette /ˈetɪket/	n.		the set of rules or customs that control accepted behaviour in particular social groups or social situations 礼节；礼仪
constant /ˈkɒntənt/	adj.		happening a lot or all the time 始终如一的；坚定的；忠实的
quote /kwəʊt/	n.		(informal for quotation) a phrase or short piece of writing taken from a longer work of literature, poetry, etc. or what someone else has said 引语，引文
icebreaker /ˈaɪsˌbreɪkə/	n.		1) something that you say or do to make people less nervous when they first meet 打破僵局的话语或行为 2) a strong ship that can break a passage through ice 破冰船
base on			使建立在……基础上
depend on			依靠；信赖
on equal ground			平等地
eye to eye			眼对眼的
in addition			另外；此外；加之

Notes

1. *Here it is, the all-important moment your palms have been sweating about.* 是时候了，你为之焦虑不安而又最重要的时刻到了。

    当将 here 或 there 提前至句首时，一般要对句子加以倒装；此句中的 Here it is 是部分倒装，作为一种强调句式，有加强语气的作用。

2. *The stage is all yours—insight into you—for a great impact and impression!* 这是你的舞台，要洞察自我，展现自我风采和魅力。

    此句中 be all yours 的意思是"都是你的；全部属于你"，表达的语气很强烈。

3. *Always remember that the introduction's sole purpose is to let all those involved and being introduced know who is who.* 时刻牢记介绍的唯一目的是让所有在场的人和被介绍的人能相互认识和了解。

    此句中的 all those involved and being introduced 是省略结构，其完整的形式是 all those who are involved and (all those who are) being introduced，是由 and 连接的并列结构，后面结构中相同的成分被省略，使得语言形式上更简洁。

    此句中的 who is who 做 know 的宾语，前一个 who 是主格，后一个 who 是宾格；直译为"谁是谁"，和中文的表达类似，但在意义上，前者指"被介绍的某人"，后者则指"（这人）是干什么的"。

4. *... you are starting from a baseline position where they have no experience of who you are or what you are like.* 你是基于这样一个情况（做自我介绍），你的观众并不了解你是谁，也不知道你是什么样的人。

    此句中的 who you are 和 what you are like 是 or 连接的并列结构，做 of 的宾语。

5. *Remember it has been rightly said that no matter what you are doing or where you are going, you are always the constant.* 要记住有句老话说得好：不管你干什么，也不管你去向何方，你都永远是你自己。

    此句中的 it 是形式主语，真实主语是 that 引导的主语从句。在这个从句中，no matter 所连接的句式是由 or 连接的并列结构，其完整形式应该是 no matter what you are doing or (no matter) where you are going。翻译上的句式应该是"不管……，也不管……"。

6. *There you go, easy peasy!* 快行动吧，很容易的一件事。

    easy peasy 完整的写法是 easy peasy, lemon squeesy，一个俗语，一般见于儿童语言场合，是"非常非常简单"的意思（something very easy and simple），有时也直接说成 easy-peasy。

Reading Comprehension

I. Answer the following questions according to the text.

1. What is the purpose of making self-introduction?

2. What topics can we take for making the self-introduction?

3. How to prepare a great self-introduction?

4. What practical steps, according to the author, are important for self-introduction?

5. Why do we have to pay careful attention to the introduction speech?

II. Choose the best answer for each of the following questions according to the text.

1. Where can we possibly make self-introduction to every other people presented?
    A. At a team building conference.
    B. Over a telephone conversation.
    C. In a school library.
    D. During a concert.

2. What is the purpose for introducing yourself?
    A. To let all those people involved and you know each other.
    B. To let all those people involved notice your appearance.
    C. To let all those people involved accept your opinions.
    D. To let all those people involved listen to you.

3. What is the first count for preparing introduction topics?
    A. Your age and the composition of your audience.
    B. Your appearance for making introduction.
    C. Your purpose of making introduction.
    D. Your speech for making introduction.

4. What kind of topics can you select to include in your introduction?
    A. Educational background.
    B. Family relationship.
    C. Future marriage.
    D. Meaning of life.

5. Why should you be careful to the introduction speech?
    A. You will never make your audience embarrassed or upset.
    B. You and your audience are on the equal ground.
    C. Your audience may not understand your speech.
    D. Your audience are not interested in your story.

Vocabulary and Structures

I. Find the definition in Column B that matches the words in Column A.

Column A	Column B
1. palm	A. the inside surface of your hand, in which you hold things
2. sweat	B. polite ways of behaving in social situations
3. impact	C. the effect or influence that an event, situation etc has on someone or something
4. critical	D. something is very important because what happens in the future depends on it
5. ensure	E. to make certain that something will happen properly
6. boastful	F. talking too proudly about yourself
7. baseline	G. a standard measurement or fact against which other measurements or facts are compared, especially in medicine or science
8. manners	H. to have drops of salty liquid coming out through your skin because you are hot, ill, frightened, or doing exercise

II. Make the best choice to fill in the blanks with the given options in the box.

A. choose a few main areas of your life with a few key ideas on them
B. the introduction's sole purpose is to let all those involved know each other
C. paying careful attention to your speech and to your manners
D. introduction's key function aims at gaining more social experience
E. where they have no experience of who you are or what you are like

　　Everyone wants to make a good first impression by making a winning self-introduction. When you are making a personal introduction or being introduced, always remember that 1) _____ . And for your personal introduction, you cannot tell your audience everything about yourself. So, 2) _____ . Self-introduction is also the key to go success, because you are starting from a baseline position 3) _____ . You may take some basic steps to ensure great introductions, such as, standing up or leaning down, showing confidence, smiling to offer a firm handshake, 4) _____ , these are very important moves for your success in good self-introductions.

Text B

Pre-reading Task: Answer the following questions before reading the text.

1. Why is making introductions important in our daily life?

2. Can you exactly describe the way of introducing one person to another?

3. How do you usually make response when you are introduced to others?

I'd Like for You to Meet Mr. Raynes

Introducing people can be one of the most important social skills you ever **master**, and making introductions can be a cause of great **distress** for some people, because they may worry that their introduction might be **handled** incorrectly.[1] We have some pieces of helpful advice that should help you in making introductions in almost any situation.

Introducing one person to another

The last should be first. When making introductions, the younger of the two or more being introduced should be introduced to the elder.[2] Using the elder's name first you might say something along these lines: "Grandmother, I would like for you to meet my favorite teacher Mrs. Daggs." What if you don't know who is older? Great question. If this is not **apparent**, **definitely** do not ask either of them his or her age. Just make a guess and introduce them using the same rule as above.

Be sure to **pronunciate** well in your speech. Whenever you are making an introduction, you should be confident and clear in your speech. Use an **adult**'s title and last name when and if you know it. **For instance**, you would make the following introduction in a meeting of your mother and your baseball coach. "Mom, this is my **baseball coach**, Mr. Herman." You might even want to add a bit of **extra** information that will help people make the connection. In the setting above you might add: "He is the one I told you about who gave me his **signed** Babe Ruth[3] baseball."

This will also enable them to have a talking point between them that is **independent** of your introduction.[4] This **principle applies to** business introductions as well. Introduce your unemployed friend to the sales manager at your dinner party adding a little extra information so that they might **strike up** a **beneficial** conversation.[5]

Introduce anyway. There will undoubtedly be times when you are in the uncomfortable embarrassment of having to introduce someone whose name you have forgotten. In this case you should first re-introduce yourself and then your acquaintance. This introduction should go something like this: "I am sorry, I know that we met last

---

master *v.* 精通，掌握
distress *v.* 使苦恼，使忧伤
handle *v.* 对待，处理

apparent *adj.* 明显的，清楚的
definitely *adv.* 明确地；肯定地
pronunciate *v.* 发音，读法

adult *n.* 成年人
for instance 例如，譬如

baseball *n.* 棒球
coach *n.* 教练
extra *adj.* 额外的；外加的
sign *v.* 签（名）

independent *adj.* 独立的，自治的
principle *n.* 原则；原理
apply to 适用于；运用
strike up 开始（交谈），建立起（友谊等）
beneficial *adj.* 有益的；有利的

year at the New Year's **Eve** ball but I can't seem to **recall** your name. My name is Grace and this is my sister Hazel."

What about when I am being introduced?

When you are being introduced to another person, you should follow the same rules that you would during self-introduction. Whenever you are being introduced you should stand, or face the person if you are already standing. If you are being introduced to someone who is seated, for instance, and elderly person or someone in a **wheelchair**, you should lean down making yourself as level with the person as possible.[6]

While you are being introduced, you should always be sure to make **eye contact**. That means look him or her in the eye and smile. If you want to make friends, show yourself friendly. In **response** to your introduction, it is good to say something simple and **straightforward**. You might try: "I am pleased to meet you, Mr. Blair."

Extend your hand and be sure to give a firm shake. This is a hand extended in friendship. In the **medieval** times it was difficult to know who was friend and who was enemy. This was because the men were often covered in **armor** from head to toe.[7] A right hand was extended in order to show the other person that there was no weapon in it and that this person was willing to be friendly. The gesture would then be returned and the greeting of friends would be completed.

Make a great first impression

Here are some last thoughts on how to **avoid** making a bad first impression. These are your takeaway-don't-do moves. Don't avoid eye contact. This action **communicates confusing** messages. It may leave the person wondering if you are **trustworthy**, or you might even appear weak, **lacking** confidence. Return the handshake. Refusing someone's hand is rude. If you are wearing gloves, remove the one on your right hand out of respect. Offer a firm shake but not one that leaves the person **wincing** in pain. Neither should you offer a limp handshake that communicates weakness.

Making introductions is a very important part of etiquette both at home and in the business **sector**. Whenever you make someone's acquaintance, you should take the time to do so properly so that you are remembered **fondly**, and perhaps called upon to enjoy parties, attend functions or **render** a service.[8] An introduction can either make or break a **relationship**.

(780 words)

Eve *n.* 前一天，前夕
recall *v.* 回想，回忆

wheelchair *n.* 轮椅

eye contact 眼神交流
response *n.* 回答；反应
straightforward *adj.* 简单的；易懂的
extend *v.* 延长，延伸；伸出
medieval *adj.* 中世纪的

armor *n.* 盔甲

avoid *v.* 避开，躲开

communicate *v.* 沟通，交流
confusing *adj.* 令人困惑的
trustworthy *adj.* 值得信赖的，可靠的
lack *v.* 缺少，缺乏
wince *v.* 畏缩；退避

sector *n.* 部分；部门

fondly *adv.* 深情地
render *v.* 给予，提供
relationship *n.* 关系

Notes

1. **... and making introductions can be a cause of great distress for some people, because they may worry that their introduction might be handled incorrectly.** ……对有些人而言，做介绍可能会给他们带来极大的焦虑，因为他们可能会担心自己不能正确处理好做介绍的事宜。

    此句中 making introductions 做主句的主语；because 引导的原因状语从句中的主语 they 指代上文的 some people；worry 后接 that 引导的宾语从句。

2. **The last should be first. When making introductions, the younger of the two or more being introduced should be introduced to the elder.** 把年纪较轻者引荐给年长者。当介绍别人的时候，要把两人或多人中较年轻的人向年长的人做介绍。

    The last should be first 这句话在文章中的意思是"把年轻的介绍给年长的"。句中 last 的本义是"最后的；末尾的"，在此句中 the last 理解为"两人或多人中最年轻的那个人"。

3. **Babe Ruth** 即乔治•赫曼。"贝比"•鲁斯（George Herman "Babe" Ruth, Jr.）是美国棒坛传奇人物，美国职业棒球当今最伟大的球员之一，曾带领纽约扬基队取得多次世界大赛冠军。

4. **This will also enable them to have a talking point between them that is independent of your introduction.** 这也能促使他们在你介绍的内容之外还有话可谈。

    此句中 a talking point between them 后接 that 引导的定语从句，定语从句修饰的先行词是名词短语结构 a talking point between them，其中介词短语 between them 做 a talking point 的后置定语。

5. **Introduce your unemployed friend to the sales manager at your dinner party adding a little extra information so that they might strike up a beneficial conversation.** 在晚宴上将待业的友人介绍给一位销售经理，介绍时多说点信息，这样可以使他们展开对双方都有收益的商谈。

    adding a little extra information 结构中的 adding 是 v-ing 形式，这个形式可以理解为其表达的动作与谓语动词 introduce 的动作同时发生，意思是"在介绍的当时多补充些（相关）信息"。

6. **If you are being introduced to someone who is seated, for instance, and elderly person or someone in a wheelchair, you should lean down making yourself as level with the person as possible.** 如果你被介绍给一位坐着的年长者或者坐在轮椅上的老人，你应该尽可能地弯下腰和对方处于同一高度来谈话。

    此句中 someone 后接 who 引导的定语从句是一并列结构，其完整的句式可以理解为 someone who is seated and (who is) elderly person or someone (who is) in a wheelchair。

7. **This was because the men were often covered in armor from head to toe.** 这是因为那个时候男士们都身披铠甲。

    from head to toe 意思是"从头到脚"，借指"全身都被铠甲覆盖，保护严密"。

8. **Whenever you make someone's acquaintance, you should take the time to do so properly so that you are remembered fondly, and perhaps called upon to enjoy parties, attend functions or render a service.** 无论你什么时候交朋结友，你都应该抓住时机好好表现，这样人们才能牢牢地记住你，甚至可能会邀请你参加朋友聚会、重要会议或提供服务。

    function 此处特指官方的或者正式的、比较大型的社交集会。

Reading Comprehension

Decide whether the following statements are true (T) or false (F) according to the text.

( ) 1. When making introductions, the younger being introduced should be introduced to the elder.

( ) 2. When making introductions, adding a bit of extra descriptive information may be not impolite.

( ) 3. When having to introduce someone whose name you have forgotten, the best way is not to say a word.

( ) 4. When being introduced to someone who is in a wheelchair, you should lean down making yourself eye to eye with the person as possible.

( ) 5. While you are being introduced you should always be sure to make eye contact.

Vocabulary

Fill in the blanks with the given words or expressions. Change the form where necessary.

1. She possesses complete technical _____ of her music instrument. (master)
2. As I _____ now, it was you who suggested this idea in the first place. (recall)
3. The exhibition has received some positive _____ from visitors. (response)
4. The River Nile _____ as far south as Lake Victoria. (extend)
5. I always _____ you with your sister—you looked so alike. (confuse)
6. The blow to his head was strong enough _____ him unconscious. (render)
7. Sandra _____ because of the pain as the dentist started to drill. (wince)
8. What I am saying only _____ some of your students. (apply to)

Section C / Extending Your English

I. Approaching the reading skill: understanding main points and supporting details（理解文章主旨要义）

一、主旨要义

主旨要义（main idea）一般是指文章的中心思想（controlling idea），或者指文章的中心论点（general point）。简言之，主旨要义就是指文章作者围绕文章主题所要阐述的主要观点，即作者想让读者通过阅读文章所能了解到的主要思想和观点。

作者通常会在文章的导入段或起首段（introductory paragraph）阐明主旨要义，所以要辨明文章的主旨要义，最简单的方法是思考并回答"What is the author telling me about this topic?"或者"What does the author want me to remember about this topic?"，然后去文章中寻找能

够回答这两个问题的句子，这样就能找到文章的主旨要义，在确定文章的主旨要义后，也就能相对简单地了解到文章的细节，以及新的词汇和文章的篇章结构。

不过在有些文章中，主旨要义并没有明确表达出来，而是隐含在文章中。作者通常会在行文中提供足够的细节和信息，而读者通过阅读这些细节和信息可以推断出并没有在文章中明示的主旨要义。

二、辅助段落的构成要素及作用

一篇文章中导入段之后的段落称为辅助段落（supporting paragraphs），通常情况下每个辅助段落都呈现一个段落中心思想来支持整个文章的主旨要义。该段落会呈现若干细节论述汇成段落中心思想（supporting point）。此外，大部分的段落都会有一个总结句（concluding sentence）来归纳和强调段落中心思想。如果读者了解了辅助段落的构成要素，就更容易了解段落中包含的信息。

1. 了解段落中心思想

如前所述，在绝大多数文章中，每一辅助段落都借助段落中心思想来支持全文主旨要义，所以要了解作者到底想说什么，就须了解这些段落中心思想。作者的观点通常在每段的首句中表述，所以段首句也被称之为"主题句"。不过，有时段落中心思想也是隐含的，需要借助段落中的句子逐步汇成段落中心思想。

2. 了解细节

除了最后的结论段外，作者在每个段落都运用细节来支持主题句。作者需要选择合适的细节来向读者清晰地表述段落大意。这些细节可能包括：

例证（specific examples）
数据（statistics）
引用（quotations）
解释（explanations）

3. 结论句

大部分的段落都会使用最后一句作为结论句（concluding sentence），用来归纳和强调段落中心思想。特别是当主题句的意义隐含时，理解结论句就显得尤为重要。在很多情况下，读者甚至不需要通读整个段落，而只通过看结论句就能把握作者想要表达的意思。

Practice: Study the following passage to understand clearly how the main idea is developed and details are used.

For many people, fashion has become an important part of their lives. People want to be fashionable so that they will impress other people. Some people believe that if they are wearing the latest designer sweater, their friends and even strangers on the street will take notice of them, and admire their taste. Being fashionable is important for people because it makes them feel good about themselves. Many people believe that wearing up-to-date clothing makes them more confident, more sure of themselves. Finally, some people think that being fashionable puts them in a higher social class. Often at times people believe if they wear expensive, high fashion clothes, they can move in a more glamorous circle of friends, and become part of the rich crowd. People seem to think fashion can do all sorts of things for them.

在这篇短文中，主旨要义是通过短文的第一个句子表述出来的，这个句子就是主题句。

Main point: Fashion is important to many people.

在文中，除主题句外，其他的句子包含有细节并支持主旨要义，作者通过使用例证的方式来支持主旨要义。

Supporting details: 1) makes them feel good about themselves
2) makes them think they are impressing others
3) makes them think they can become part of the rich crowd

II. Applying the reading skill

Read the following passage and do the exercises.

Outdated? —Only Introduce Men to Women

In the U.S., there has been a **longstanding** social rule that men should be introduced to women first. However, in the workplace, women have the same rights and respect as men. So does this "introduce men to women" rule still apply? **Technically**, no, at least not in business.

Challenge the Outdated Social Rules: Is It about the Rights or Business?

Here remains a sad fact: any time a woman **claims** her rights to be equal to men in a business settings, it can sometimes work against her, and may bring bad impact on her **career**. So to get get rid of any problem—even outdated social rules, is usually the better way to **accomplish** something.

For a business woman, the best advice is: put your business **ahead of** your own **ego**. Choose the best introduction to accomplish your **goals** for success: to build strong business relationships. Do not use an introduction to take a political attitude on women's rights—unless that is your **primary** business goal. As "wrong" as this will sound to some women, if you cannot get your foot in the door, you will never take the Board room or a **men-dominated** industry.[1]

Forget the Gender Neutral Rule: Is It Business or Personal?

Even men have to "play the game" in business to get ahead, rather than thinking of introductions as having to be **gender-neutral** to be fair. Women may apply a different rule for introductions: If it is a business setting—put your business first—not your gender.

We are not in any way suggesting women should lower

---

longstanding *adj.* 长期存在的

technically *adv.* 技术上

challenge *v.* 质疑；挑战
outdated *adj.* 过时的，旧式的
claim *v.* 声称；断言

career *n.* 职业；事业

accomplish *v.* 完成；达到（目的）

ahead of 在……之前
ego *n.* 自我；自负
goal *n.* 目标，目的
primary *adj.* 首要的，主要的

men-dominated *adj.* 男性占首要地位的

gender-neutral *adj.* 中性的

themselves to men in any business environment. However, women in business have to learn one of the most **valuable** lessons in life long ago: Choose your battles wisely to gain the most control.² Not every little thing in life is worth fighting over in any given moment; timing is everything.

One question to consider is, "Do you want to be seen as a business woman that is equal to men, or truly gender neutral and simply as a business **professional**?" For every woman, this is a personal choice she must be comfortable with, and not one decided for her by social rules, or even by other women.³

Still Not Sure What to do about Introductions?

Bear in mind, however, that in business, it is all about social **networking**, and introduction is a big factor in successfully networking yourself and your business.　　　　　　　(410 words)

valuable *adj.* 贵重的，宝贵的；有价值的

professional *n.* 专业人士

bear in mind 牢记
networking *n.* 人际关系网
（network *v.* 为……建立人际关系网）

Notes

1. *As "wrong" as this will sound to some women, if you cannot get your foot in the door, you will never take the Board room or a men-dominated industry.* 对有些女士而言，这个听起来不对。但是如果你不能走出第一步，你就永远都不可能执掌高层或者掌管男士主控的行业。

    get a foot in the door 意为"迈出第一步"。

    以前美国的推销员挨家挨户地去推销商品。当一位家庭主妇把门打开的时候，精明的推销员就会把一只脚先伸到门里边，这样可以避免在介绍他的商品之前女主人就把门关上。get a foot in the door 这个说法后来成了一个常用的俗语，其意思也演变成了"为了达到某个目的而迈出第一步"。

2. *Choose your battles wisely to gain the most control.* 灵活应战，掌控全局。

3. *For every woman, this is a personal choice she must be comfortable with, and not one decided for her by social rules, or even by other women.* 对每位女士而言，这是个她应该欣然做出的个人抉择，这个抉择既不是通过社会规约迫使她做出，更不是其他女性强迫她做出的。

    … she must be comfortable with 为省略关系代词的定语从句修饰 a personal choice，由于关系代词在从句中做介词 with 的宾语，故此省略 and 后接一个并列的句子 not one decided for her...，并列句中的 one 为不定代词，指代 choice。

Exercise 1. Read the introductory paragraph and mark an (√) beside the sentence which you think answers the question "what point does the author want to make in this reading?".

_____ "Introduce men to women" rule still gains popularity in American society.

_____ "Introduce men to women" rule is now socially out of use in the U.S.

_____ "Introduce men to women" rule becomes less applicable in business circle.

Reading Skills

Exercise 2. Finish reading paragraph 2 and paragraph 3 of the passage. Ask yourself, "What are the main points the author wants us to know from supporting paragraphs?" State your answer in complete sentences.

Paragraph 2 _____

_____

_____

Paragraph 3 _____

_____

_____

Section D / Self-evaluation

After learning this unit, I have grasped

Items \ %	100%	80%	60%	Below 50%
Words				
Grammar				
Reading				

Notes to this unit:

Unit 2

Job Interview

Learning Objectives

In this unit, you will learn

- to prepare for a job interview;
- to get basic information about the types of job interview;
- to master the new words and expressions related to job interview;
- to apply the reading skill—understanding the text organization.

Section A / Lead-in

I. Can you name these types of job interview?

Directions: Match the words or expressions in the box with the pictures.

（1）

（2）

（3）

（4）

（5）

（6）

A. Telephone Interview   B. Video Interview   C. One-on-one Interview
D. Panel Interview   E. Group Interview   F. Career Fair Interview

II. Describe the above pictures.

Directions: Work in pairs to describe the type of job interview you are most familiar with.

Section B / Embracing English

Text A

Pre-reading Task: Answer the following questions before reading the text.

1. Have you ever taken any job interview? What questions did you have in the interview?

2. How can one prepare for a job interview?

3. What questions may be asked at a job interview?

Sharing My Job Interview Experience

It is said that an **awesome résumé** gets you an interview, and a **successful** interview gets you an offer. Indeed, interviewing is an important skill. It involves not only expressing yourself clearly, but also communicating it to your interviewer. As a graduate student, I have had several interview experiences. There are mistakes and some shining points in those experiences that I would like to share now.

About two years ago, I had a phone interview with a big **local accounting** company for a tax **internship opportunity**. Because this was my first formal interview, I did a lot of homework. I checked through the possible interview questions and prepared answers, while also researching the company's **background**. I found the WikiJob[1] website was quite useful for me during my **preparation**.

It took me a whole day to prepare myself. Even so, my voice was still shaking when the interview began. "Tell me about yourself in one minute. Give me an example of yourself as a team leader." I answered these questions **without hesitation** because I already had them on my **cheat sheet**. Then the interviewer asked, "Why would you like to join our company?" I answered her question from both **professional** advantage and **social responsibility** of the company. She seemed to be satisfied with my performance so far.

"Great, now tell me about one of your biggest weaknesses." I didn't expect this question. I remembered clearly that it was among the questions list, but I didn't prepare for this one. "Err… I am a …" This is not an easy question, because these weaknesses may prevent the interviewer from hiring me. After a long pause, I decided to say what came to my mind first: "I am a quick person, when something isn't done in time, I would get worried and try to finish it as soon as possible."

When I finished this sentence, I realized that I had lost this opportunity. You may not get a job even if you provide many excellent answers, but you can certainly ruin it with only one weak response. After that interview I had a talk with my career coach and she said, "**Take** these interview questions **seriously** and prepare every one of them well. Only so could you know yourself as an interviewee[2]. You may still meet some questions that you never expected before. Don't worry at this point; try to bring those answers you already know to prove that you are the person they are looking for."

A couple of months ago, I got invited to interview with a well-known **not-for-profit organization**. I was so eager to get this internship that I even bought a new suit for the interview. I read a lot of articles about the organization's **mission**, history and values. I tried to contact an **alumnus** working in the organization to get a reference. I researched my interviewers, including their educational background and past work experience. Lastly, I went through my prepared responses for common interview questions to make sure that I would not make serious mistakes.

When the day came, the new suit was still at the tailor's shop. However, it didn't affect me much. I knew I was **adequately** prepared, so I wasn't nervous at all. I did well at the beginning, answering questions about myself and telling them what I knew about the organization. After that, my interviewers and I talked about life in New York, my **referrer**, and a lot of other little things. It was more like a chat than an interview.

"Well, I can get this job," I told myself after walking out of the building. As I expected, I received my offer letter two weeks later.

There is a very famous Chinese **proverb** which states, "**Precise** knowledge of self and precise knowledge of the **threat** leads to victory."³ You should not consider the interviewer an enemy; however, it is a perfect **metaphor** for an interview. Know yourself, know your interviewer, and know that you may never prepare too much for your interviews.

(669 words)

New Words and Expressions

awesome /'ɔːsəm/	adj.	very good 极好的	
résumé /'rezjumeɪ/	n.	a short written account of your education and your previous jobs that you send to an employer when you are looking for a new job (= CV British English) 〈美〉履历，简历	
successful /sək'sesfəl/	adj.	having the effect or result you intended 成功的	
local /'ləʊkəl/	adj	relating to the particular area you live in, or the area you are talking about 当地的，本地的	
accounting /ə'kaʊntɪŋ/	n.	the measurement, processing and communication of financial information about economic entities 会计	
internship /'ɪntɜːnʃɪp/	n.	a job that lasts for a short time, that someone, especially a student, does in order to gain experience 实习，实习岗位	
opportunity /ˌɔpə'tjuːnɪti/	n.	a chance to do something or an occasion when it is easy for you to do something 机会，时机	
background /'bækgraʊnd/	n.	the situation or past events that explain why something happens in the way that it does 背景	
preparation /ˌprepə'reɪʃən/	n.	the process of preparing something 准备	
professional /prə'feʃənəl/	adj.	relating to a job that needs special education and training 职业的，专业的	
mission /'mɪʃən/	n.	something that you feel you must do because it is your duty 使命，天职	
alumnus /ə'lʌmnəs/	n.	a former student of a school, college, etc. 校友	
adequately /'ædɪkwɪtli/	adv.	enough in quantity or of a good enough quality for a particular purpose 足够地，充分地	
referrer /rɪ'fɜːrə/	n.	someone who provides information about you when you are trying to get a job 推荐人；介绍人	
proverb /'prɔvɜːb/	n.	a short well-known statement that gives advice or expresses something that is generally true 谚语，格言	

precise /prɪˈsaɪs/		*adj.*	exact, clear, and correct 精确的，准确的
threat /θret/		*n.*	someone or something that is regarded as a possible danger 威胁
metaphor /ˈmetəfə/		*n.*	a way of describing something by referring to it as something different and suggesting that it has similar qualities to that thing 暗喻；比喻
without hesitation			毫不犹豫地，不假思索地
cheat sheet			小抄，备忘单
social responsibility			社会责任
take… seriously			认真对待……
not-for-profit organization			非营利性机构

Notes

1. WikiJob 英国一家商业网站，主要为毕业生提供就业信息和咨询服务：http://www.wikijob.co.uk。
2. *Only so could you know yourself as an interviewee.* 只有这样你才能认清自己作为一个来参加面试的人的身份。

   本句为倒装句。副词 only 放在句首时，对时间、地点、条件、方式等状语加以强调，在这种情况下，句子要改为倒装语序。副词 so 表示方式，意为"这样做"，指的是上句中提到的"take these interview questions seriously and prepare every one of them well."
3. *There is a very famous Chinese proverb which states, "Precise knowledge of self and precise knowledge of the threat leads to victory."* 中国有句名言："知彼知己，百战不殆"。

   此话出自《孙子兵法》中的《谋攻篇》。2003 年伊拉克战争前，美军战场总指挥、中央司令部司令汤米·R. 弗兰克斯（Tommy R. Franks）曾这样引用过"知彼知己，百战不殆"这句话。

Reading Comprehension

I. Answer the following questions according to the text.

1. What does the author think of the role of "interviewing"?

2. How many job interviews does the author share with us? What were they and how were the results?

3. What "homework" did the author do before his first job interview?

4. How did the career coach advise him?

5. What experience does the author get from his own job interviews?

Reading Skills

II. Choose the best answer for each of the following questions according to the text.

1. Where did the author have his first formal job interview?
   A. In a firm.
   B. On a website.
   C. On the phone.
   D. In a job fair.

2. How did the author feel when he began taking the first interview?
   A. Calm.
   B. Nervous.
   C. Excited.
   D. Relaxed.

3. Why did the author think he lost the internship opportunity with the accounting firm?
   A. Because he didn't have any work experience.
   B. Because he didn't know well about the company.
   C. Because he didn't take the career coach's advice.
   D. Because he didn't give a good answer to an interview question.

4. In preparing for the interview with the not-for-profit organization, why did the author contact an alumnus?
   A. To get his recommendation.
   B. To get a new suit from him.
   C. To get some articles from him.
   D. To get his past work experience.

5. Why did the author believe he could get the job after walking out of the building?
   A. Because he was not nervous.
   B. Because he was dressed properly in the new suit.
   C. Because one of the interviewers was his alumnus.
   D. Because he prepared well for the interview and performed well at it.

Vocabulary and Structures

I. Find the definition in Column B that matches the words in Column A.

Column A	Column B
1. successful	A. favorable time, occasion or set of circumstances
2. local	B. having succeeded or being marked by a favorable outcome
3. opportunity	C. stated clearly and accurately
4. preparation	D. belonging to a particular place or district
5. mission	E. person or thing regarded as likely to cause danger or ruin
6. precise	F. have an influence on (somebody/something); produce an effect on
7. threat	G. particular task or duty undertaken by an individual or a group
8. affect	H. the activity of putting or setting in order in advance of some act or purpose

II. Make the best choice to fill in the blanks with the given options in the box.

> A. felt confident and relaxed at the interview
> B. performed very poorly at it
> C. with a not-for-profit organization
> D. I still failed to get the offer
> E. with an accounting company

I have learned from my own job interview experiences that interviewing skills are very important. And I would like to share my experiences. My first formal interview was a phone interview 1) _____ for an internship position. I prepared a lot for that and did well at the beginning of the interview, but 2) _____ when I gave a weak response to an unprepared question. Another time, I got an interview opportunity for an internship 3) _____ . This time, I made more and better preparations and 4) _____ . Naturally, I succeeded in it. From such experiences, I have realized that an interviewee should know both himself and the interviewer very well and always prepare well for the interview so as to get the job.

Text B

Pre-reading Task: Answer the following questions before reading the text.

1. Can you name some types of job interviews?

2. Which type of job interview do you think is easiest for you? Why?

3. Which type of job interview do you think is most difficult for you? Why?

Some Common Types of Job Interviews

Like people, job interviews come **in all shapes and sizes**. Like people, job interviews can be difficult. Like people, job interviews can suffer from lots of pressure.[1] Before you go on your interview, you will surely want to know what type of job interview you will take ahead of time. Don't be afraid to ask your employer what type the interview will be, as it serves both of you and the interviewer. Whether you know the type of interview or not **beforehand**, it is a good idea to **brush up on** the types of job

> in all shapes and sizes 以各种形式，各式各样
>
> beforehand adv. 提前，预先
> brush up on 复习，重温

interviews that the employers may use so that you can be ready for any interview.[2]

The **one-on-one interview**[3] is one of the most common types of job interviews where you meet one **representative** of the company, most likely the manager of the position you are applying for. Because you will be working with this person directly if you get the job, he or she will want to get a feel for who you are and if your skills match those of the job requirements. Many times the interviewer will ask you questions about the experience and skills, what you can offer to the company or position.

In a **panel interview**, the job **applicant** is interviewed by several people from the company. The panel may **consist of** a variety of members, such as the hiring manager, your future direct manager, and other involved parties. Panel interviews are known to be very hard, but take it easy! If you prepare well, it should be a piece of cake. You'll have **a variety of** questions coming at you during a panel interview. Stay cool and calm by taking one question at a time and make eye contact when answering each question.

In a **group interview**, you will be along with other candidates at the same time for the same position. This is your chance to show your **leadership potential**, communication skills and how well you work with others. Sometimes, you may even be asked to **solve** a problem as a team. This allows the interviewers to help determine if you are **reserved**, **pushy** or have a **balance** between offering and listening to ideas. This is perhaps one of the most difficult interviews and it is easy to get lost in the rest of the faces.[4] To do well in such interviews, remember to speak to everybody in the group with respect, **regardless of** how much they are doing to the cause. Always be polite even if other people are not. Do your best to avoid power struggles. They will only result in the interviewers forming a **negative** opinion about you.

A **phone interview** is often the first round for an open position. It's cost effective and often lasts from 10 to 30 minutes. The great thing about phone interviews is that you can have notes in front of you: your resume and CV, information about the job and the company, your list of references, and any answers you've prepared.[5] Your answers need to be **polished** (so practice ahead of time with a friend or family member if you're not great at interviews) and you should **convey** interest in the job. Remember,

---

representative *n.* 代表

panel *n.* 专门小组
applicant *n.* 申请人，求职者
consist of 由……组成

a variety of 各种各样的

leadership *n.* 领导能力
potential *n.* 潜力，潜能
solve *v.* 解决，解答
reserved *adj.* 内向的，矜持的
pushy *adj.* 有进取心的
balance *n.* 平衡，均衡

regardless of 不管，不顾

negative *adj.* 否定的，负面的

polish *v.* 修正，改进

convey *v.* 表达，传达

the employer cannot see you, so you need to sell yourself effectively through your words and tone of voice. By the way, you'd better get dressed. Studies have shown that people dressed professionally for a phone interview will perform better than those dressed **casually**.

Video interviews are becoming more common for busy employers and distant job applicants, as hiring becomes more international. Video interviews are usually used in one of two ways on the Internet: in real-time by Skype or **video conferencing software** or recorded and sent to the company using video interview **software**.[6] Video interviews can seem frightening to job seekers, but prepare for them as usual. Be early, wear professional suit, and research yourself and the company before the interview. If you have any trouble with software or technology, don't be shy to ask for help.

A *career fair interview* could be a conversation during a career fair. It is often 2-10 minutes in length with a HR manager or a technical director in your field. If **mutual** interest is built up, it is likely that you will be invited for further interviews. Because your meeting is short, you will need to make an immediate good impression. Research the employer and match your background and interests to their needs.

No matter what you learn about each particular interview type, there are some **similarities** between all of them—**predict** questions, develop your answers and practice makes perfect. Articles such as this one and others can give you directions, but you need to learn how to **adapt** them to yourself. And remember to sell yourself, your qualifications and your skills at all times.

(806 words)

casually *adv.* 随意地，休闲地

video conferencing 视频会议，电视会议
software *n.* 软件

mutual *adj.* 相互的；共同的

similarity *n.* 相似点，相似之处
predict *v.* 预测，预言

adapt *v.* 使适应

Notes

1. *Like people, job interviews come in all shapes and sizes. Like people, job interviews can be difficult. Like people, job interviews can suffer from lots of pressure.* 人有形形色色，工作面试也有各式各样；人不易相处，工作面试也难应付；人有重重压力，工作面试也会遭遇压力重重。

    文章开篇采用三个句子结构相似的排比句式，将 job interviews 和 people 做了一个类比，形象地描述了工作面试形式多样、不容易应对的特点。

2. *Whether you know the type of interview or not beforehand, it is a good idea to brush up on the types of job interviews that the employers may use so that you can be ready for any interview.* 不论你是否事先知道面试的形式，温习一下招聘人员可能采用的面试的各种类型，以便你自己做好准

备，总是一个不错的办法。

此句中 Whether ... or not 结构引导一个让步状语从句"不论……"；主句中 it 做形式主语，动词不定式短语 to brush up on ... 是真正的主语，so that... 引导的目的状语从句说明这样做的目的，that 引导的定语从句修饰 the types of job interviews。

3. one-on-one interview 　一对一面试
   panel interview 　　　小组面试
   group interview 　　　集体面试
   phone interview 　　　电话面试
   video interview 　　　视频面试
   career fair interview 招聘会面试

4. *This is perhaps one of the most difficult interviews and it is easy to get lost in the rest of the faces.* 这或许是最难的面试形式之一了，因为你很难从其他参加面试的人中脱颖而出。

   此并列句的第二个分句中 it 同样为形式主语，动词不定式短语为真正的主语，get lost in ... 意为"在……中迷失自己"，the faces 指代那些一起参加小组面试的其他人。

5. *The great thing about phone interviews is that you can have notes in front of you: your resume and CV, information about the job and the company, your list of references, and any answers you've prepared.* 电话面试好的一点是你可以将做好的备忘记录摆在面前，包括简历、工作职位和公司的信息、推荐信以及准备好的应答内容。

   此句中，that 引导的表语从句说明主语的内容，冒号后面的几个并列名词短语说明 notes 的具体内容，其中 CV = Curriculum Vitae，意为"简历"。

6. *Video interviews are usually used in one of two ways on the Internet: in real-time by Skype or video conferencing software or recorded and sent to the company using video interview software.* 视频面试通常是在互联网上以如下两种方式进行的：用 Skype 或其他视频会议软件进行实时面试，或者是用视频面试软件先录制视频再发送给所应聘的公司。

   Skype 是一款免费的全球实时语音沟通软件。用 Skype 可以与全球用户进行免费的文字、语音、视频交流，开展电话会议，或是快速传送文件。

Reading Comprehension

Decide whether the following statements are True (T) or False (F) according to the text.

(　　) 1. It is suggested that you should not ask the employer what type of interview you would take beforehand even though you want to know.

(　　) 2. Most job applicants believe that panel interview is a piece of cake.

(　　) 3. In a group interview, you should try to take every opportunity to be the leader without paying attention to other candidates.

(　　) 4. On a phone interview, you should also be dressed professionally though the interviewer cannot see you.

(　　) 5. There are some common points between the different types of job interviews.

Vocabulary

Fill in the blanks with the given words or expressions. Change the form where necessary.

1. Many _____ of the trade union attended the meeting. (representative)
2. It is _____ that the unemployment rate will reach 7% at the end of this year. (predict)
3. With loans from the bank, the company has almost _____ its capital problem. (solve)
4. The manager spent a whole afternoon _____ the business plan. (polish)
5. The two companies eventually arrived at a figure that was _____ acceptable. (mutual)
6. For a job interview, one should wear professional instead of _____ clothes. (casually)
7. It is surprising that their products look quite _____ to those of our company? (similarity)
8. After one month of internship, I have _____ myself to the working environment. (adapt)

Section C / Extending Your English

I. Approaching the reading skill: understanding the text organization（理解文章结构）

一般来说，阅读一篇英语文章的目的是为了获取信息，而获取文章信息的最有效方法之一就是去学习和了解文章的结构，以便更加准确、快速地定位要找的信息。从宏观上讲，文章结构是指整篇文章的整体结构布局，由开篇、主体和结尾这三个部分组成，结构模式如下：

i. Introduction
  1. Interest drawing material
  2. Thesis statement
  3. (Transitional sentence)
ii. Body (More paragraphs)
  1. (Transitional sentence or phrase)
  2. Topic sentence
  3. Developments
  4. (Transitional sentence)
iii. Ending
  1. (Transitional sentence or phrase)
  2. Conclusion, summary, restatement of the thesis, etc

一、 开篇部分

开篇部分或称引言部分（Introduction），长短无定式，可以因为不同文体、不同题材、不同作者风格而有所不同。这部分的目的在于揭示主题（theme），引出文中要讨论的核心问题，从而起到统领全文的作用。通常，开篇部分由吸引读者兴趣的材料（interest drawing material）语段和主题陈述（thesis statement）语段两部分组成。前者的目的是引起读者的兴趣，同时使读者对文章要讨论的问题在心理上有所准备，后者向读者交代该文的主题或写作目的（purpose）。

总之，开篇部分的作用就是使读者顺利地进入正文。

吸引读者兴趣的材料形式可以多种多样，可以是一句惊世骇俗的论断（claim），如一位女性作者在文章第一句就说"I also want a wife"；可以是一段逸闻趣事（anecdote）；或者是发人深省的问题（issue）；也可以是名人学者的一段语录（quotation）；还可以是一个具体情景的细致生动的描述（description）。这样的材料短则一句，长则一段甚至数段。

主题陈述相当于中文所说的中心思想。但是，受中国传统文化的影响，中文作者往往讲究含蓄、隐而不露，因此中文文章的中心思想往往需要读者自己去归纳总结。英文则相反，英文文章讲究逻辑性、一致性、连贯性，讲究"重点先表达"，因而可以在开篇部分找到 thesis 的重要信息。主题陈述的特征是一个需要发展支持，可以而且实际上也被文章的主体部分发展支持的一个论断或陈述（a statement that requires development or support, one that can be, and is practically covered by the body of the essay）。

二、主体部分

主体部分（Body）一般由若干段落组成，它们主要是从不同的方面发展支持开篇部分所提出的主题陈述。各段阐述的内容必须与主题一致，有助于说明中心思想，但是每段只涉及主题的一个方面。

转折句或词语（transitional sentence or phrase）可以在某一段的段尾，起着承接下文的作用，或在某一段的段首，起着承上启下的作用。

主体部分的段落（paragraph），或称发展段，主要由本段主题句（topic sentence）及发展句（supporting sentences）构成。主题句的特征与主题陈述大同小异，是一个需要发展支持，可以而且实际上也被本段的主体部分发展支持的一个论断或陈述。主题句最多出现在段首，也可出现在段尾或段中，有时甚至没有，称为暗含的主题句（implied topic sentence）。在实际阅读中，有经验的读者会自动地（automatically）去留意表现本段主题的思想（idea）。阅读练习中，可以有重点地注意段首、段尾。

段落发展可以有一个到数个要点，依然是遵循"重点先表达，越往后越详细，后句支持前句，一个要点交代完毕转向另一个要点"的规律。在一个要点转向另一个要点时，可以出现承上启下的，表现各种关系的信号词语（signal words）。

三、结尾部分

结尾部分（Ending）通常是一个小段，一些篇幅较长的文章可以有三段甚至更多段落结尾。作者可以在此部分归纳总结全文中心思想，或得出结论，或提出建议、警告，或提出自己的"真知灼见"，或以一种不同的、更概括的、更强调的方式重申全文主题，从而与篇首段相呼应，使读者对全文有一个完整、清晰的认识。

II. Applying the reading skill

Read the following passage and fill in the blanks with the given sentences as options.

How to Prepare for a Job Interview

Job interviews can be very frightening. You're all dressed up, and you don't know how the interviewers are going to treat you. 1) _____ .

2) _____ . Learn all that you can about the company, its history of development, its goals and values, and even a little bit about their **competitors**. You can use the Internet to help look for such information. If the interviewers find that you know about them, they will have the impression that you are really interested in their company.

3) _____ . Bring one or two copies of your resume. You never know; you might be interviewed by more than one person. Bring a **notepad** and a pencil, too, and they'll know that you want to learn more about the position.

4) _____ . They will know you're interested in the job if you have questions handy. To **aid** in interview preparation, you can find several examples of questions online. But remember not to copy the ready answers; instead, you have to adapt them to your own situation.

5) _____ . Dress in your best business **attire** and your best shoes. Try everything on ahead of time so you don't have any last minute **fashion disasters**. Pay attention to **detail**—your hair, nails, shoes, should all look polished and professional.

6) _____ . Make eye contact, firmly shake hands, smile, and get ready to shine! Practice interviewing by having a friend or family member run through the whole process with you. Stay calm and know that you're ready to do your best. You've spent time practicing and preparing, so you'll be ready to interview effectively.

(355 words)

competitor *n.* 竞争者，对手

notepad *n.* 笔记本，记事手册

aid *v.* 帮助，援助

attire *n.* 衣服，服装

fashion *n.* 时装，时尚
disaster *n.* 灾难，不幸
detail *n.* 细节，详情

Options:
A. Show your interviewers that you've come prepared.
B. Your interviewers are going to ask you questions, but you need to ask questions, as well.
C. A job interview is all about presenting yourself as the best candidate for the job, so be confident.
D. If you really want the job, do research.
E. Additionally, be sure and dress to impress.
F. However, if you are going to land a job, and make the money you want, you need to be prepared for each and every interview you go on.

Section D / Self-evaluation

After learning this unit, I have grasped

Items	100%	80%	60%	Below 50%
Words				
Grammar				
Reading				

Notes to this unit:

Unit 3

A New Job

Learning Objectives

In this unit, you will learn

- to understand the importance of starting a new job;
- to get basic information about the first day at work;
- to master the new words and expressions;
- to apply the reading skill—understanding stated information.

Section A / Lead-in

I. Can you name these behaviors?

Directions: Match the words or expressions in the box with the pictures.

（1）

（2）

（3）

（4）

（5）

（6）

> A. getting distracted   B. keeping a smile   C. being impatient
> D. dressing well   E. asking questions   F. greeting colleagues

II. Describe the above pictures.

Directions: Work in pairs to describe the proper behaviors on the first day at work.

Section B / Embracing English

Text A

Pre-reading Task: Answer the following questions before reading the text.

1. Do you think the first day at a new job important? Why do you think so?

2. What should you consider the day before your first day at a new job?

3. What do you expect on the first day at a new job?

On Your First Day at a New Job

You beat out the competition to get hired for a new job. On your first day, it might feel like you are back at a starting line—which, in fact, you are.¹ It will be a busy day. You will most likely meet with the human resources department to complete **paperwork**, get settled into your **workplace**, establish computer **passwords** and much more.² But while you are taking care of all of that, you will be introduced to people who hold the keys to your success. It is completely natural to feel nervous. You are entering an unknown work environment. You think you will be able to meet the demands and **expectations** of the job, but you aren't confident.

Break the ice with colleagues by offering a warm smile and handshake. Make a good first impression. Besides, here are some other tips to help you get through the first day **with flying colors**.

First, dress well, in business style—although wearing clothes and shoes you are not comfortable in. In their article, "Your First Days Working at a New Job: 20 Tips to Help You Make a Great Impression," Randall S. Hansen and Katharine Hansen note that a new employee should dress in the manner that he wants people to perceive him.³ Being a careful dresser can show that you accept responsibility. Give colleagues a warm smile and firm handshake and look them in the eye when being introduced. Repeat their names to help you remember them. All of these steps will help you to appear ready to become a part of the team.

Second, ask questions. This shows you are eager to learn about the job and company and it helps you to become settled in the job faster. Take notes if you think you are getting more information than you can easily remember. But do not ask so many questions that you become a **nuisance** to your colleagues or boss. **Back off** if you think you might be **interfering** with work they need to finish.

Third, lay low, but pay attention, advises CBS⁴ Money Watch contributor Amy Levin-Epstein, in her article "New Job? 8 Tips For Your First Day." By paying attention to what goes on around you in the office, you can come to understand the corporate culture in your new job quickly.⁵ She **recommends** watching how people present themselves, how they work together and how they interact with the company's clients.

Fourth, apologize if you make a mistake, but do not apologize too much. Cathie Black, **former** chairman of Hearst Magazines⁶ and former New York City Schools **chancellor**, says in an interview at the First 30 Days website not to apologize **profusely** like your mistake is the end of the world. Keep in mind that everyone makes mistakes, she advises, and **simply** say that you are very sorry and will not make the mistake again.

Fifth, stay late. Staying just five to ten minutes past **quitting** time will help let colleagues and your boss know that you are not a "clock watcher" and are **committed** to your work and the company.

Actually, your first day on the job begins the evening before. Make certain your **alarm** is set to wake you up in plenty of time to arrive at your job at least five minutes early. **Lay out** your professional clothes and **accessories** to save time in the morning. Also check to make sure that they are pressed and clean.⁷

(582 words)

New Words and Expressions

paperwork /ˈpeɪpəwɜːk/   *n.*   forms or documents that need to be completed in doing business 表格；文件，资料

workplace /ˈwɜːkpleɪs/   *n.*   the room, building etc. where you work 工作场所

password /ˈpɑːswɜːd/   *n.*   a secret group of letters or numbers that you must type into a computer before you can use a system or program 口令；密码

expectation /ˌekspekˈteɪʃn/   *n.*   what you think or hope will happen 预料；期望

nuisance /ˈnjuːsns/   *n.*   a person, thing, or situation that annoys you or causes problems 讨厌的人；讨厌的东西

interfere /ˌɪntəˈfɪə(r)/   *v.*   to deliberately get involved in a situation where you are not wanted or needed 干涉；妨碍

recommend /ˌrekəˈmend/   *v.*   to advise someone to do something, especially because you have special knowledge of a situation or subject 推荐；建议

former /ˈfɔːmə(r)/   *adj.*   having a particular position in the past 前者的；以前的

chancellor /ˈtʃɑːnsələ(r)/   *n.*   the person in charge of some American universities（某些美国大学的）校长

profusely /prəˈfjuːsli/   *adv.*   produced or existing in large quantities 丰富地；大量地

simply /ˈsɪmpli/   *adv.*   only 仅仅

quit /kwɪt/   *v.*   [informal] to leave a job, school etc, especially without finishing it completely 离开；辞职

committed /kəˈmɪtɪd/   *adj.*   willing to work very hard at something 忠诚的；坚定的

alarm /əˈlɑːm/   *n.*   an alarm clock 闹钟

accessory /əkˈsesəri/   *n.*   [usually plural] something such as a bag, belt, or jewellery that you wear or carry because it is attractive（常用复数）配件；（女用手提包等的）装饰品

break the ice   打破沉默

with flying colors   出色地

back off   后退；让步

lay out   设计；安排；陈列

Notes

1. *On your first day, it might feel like you are back at a starting line—which, in fact, you are.* 上班的第一天里，你仿佛又回到了起点，而事实上的确如此。

　　which 指代的是破折号前面整句话的内容；末尾的 you are 是省略的说法，即 you are back at a starting line。

2. *You will most likely meet with the human resources department to complete paperwork, get settled into your workplace, establish computer passwords and much more.* 你很有可能和人力资源部的人见面，他们会让你填写一些表格，给你安排好工作地点，帮你设置电脑密码，等等。

   get settled into your workplace, establish computer passwords and much more 与前面的 complete paperwork 是并列的动词不定式短语，共用一个不定式符号 to。

3. *Randall S. Hansen and Katharine Hansen note that a new employee should dress in the manner that he wants people to perceive him.* 兰德尔·S. 汉森和凯瑟琳·汉森指出新雇员的着装必须能使别人注意到自己。

   这句话是多重复合句，包含两个从句。note 后面的 that 从句是作为主句的宾语；在这个宾语从句中又有一个 that 引导的定语从句，用来修饰其前面的 manner 一词。

4. CBS：Columbia Broadcasting System（美国）哥伦比亚广播公司，MoneyWatch 是该公司旗下的互动传媒公司和新闻频道下的财经栏目。

5. *By paying attention to what goes on around you in the office, you can come to understand the corporate culture in your new job quickly.* 关注办公室里发生的事情可以使你迅速地了解新工作中包含的公司文化。

   介词 by 表示"靠，通过"，它所在的部分充当方式状语。by 后面可以跟名词或动名词。what goes on around you in the office 为名词性从句，在句中作 paying attention to 的宾语。

6. Hearst Magazines 指美国出版界巨头赫斯特国际集团旗下的20余种杂志，消费类杂志是该集团最成功、最引人注目的媒体业务。

7. *Also check to make sure that they are pressed and clean.* 还要检查以确定它们（衣服）是熨好的、干净的。

   这句话和其前面的两个句子都是祈使句，它的主语是听话人（you），一般不需要说出来。通常以动词原形开头，表示请求、命令。此句中的 press 是"熨烫；熨平"的意思。

Reading Comprehension

I. Answer the following questions according to the text.

1. How does one usually feel on the first day at a new job?

2. How can we behave properly on the first day at a new job?

3. What steps help you to appear ready to become a part of the team?

4. How does Amy Levin-Epstein suggest people?

5. What should we note for our clothing on the first day at a new job?

II. Choose the best answer for each of the following questions according to the text.

1. Which of the following is NOT what you do with the human resources department on your first day at a new job?
   A. Get settled into your workplace.
   B. Complete paperwork.
   C. Get a one-month payment.
   D. Establish computer passwords.

2. According to the author, what helps you remember your colleagues' names?
   A. Take notes when your are introduced to your colleagues.
   B. Repeat their names.
   C. Input their names into your computer.
   D. Spell out their names.

3. What might happen if you ask your colleagues or boss too many questions?
   A. You will lose your job.
   B. Your colleagues or boss will be pleased.
   C. You will be praised by your colleagues or boss.
   D. Your colleagues or boss might not finish their work on time.

4. Why shouldn't you apologize too much for your mistakes?
   A. Everyone makes mistakes.
   B. Nobody cares about your mistakes.
   C. You don't feel very sorry for your mistakes.
   D. Nobody accepts your apology.

5. What is a "clock watcher"?
   A. It's an alarm clock.
   B. It's an employee who pays attention to the quitting time.
   C. It's the supervisor in the company.
   D. It's an employee who arrives at the office on time.

Vocabulary and Structures

I. Find the definition in Column B that matches the words in Column A.

Column A	Column B
1. quit	A. to leave a job, school etc., especially without finishing it completely
2. workplace	B. the room, building 'etc.' where you work
3. recommend	C. to advise someone to do something, especially because you have special knowledge of a situation or subject

4. interfere	D. to deliberately get involved in a situation where you are not wanted or needed
5. committed	E. willing to work very hard at something
6. former	F. having a particular position in the past
7. profusely	G. in an abundant manner
8. nuisance	H. a person, thing, or situation that annoys you or causes problems.

II. Make the best choice to fill in the blanks with the given options in the box.

A. you are eager to learn about the job and company
B. you accept responsibility
C. you are very sorry and will not make the mistake again
D. you might be interfering with work they need to finish
E. understand the corporate culture in your new job quickly

Your first day at a new job will be very busy. You will take care of many things and meet some important people. Break the ice with colleagues by offering a warm smile and handshake. Besides, there are some other tips you should follow. You should dress in business style because it shows that 1) _____ . Asking questions for it shows 2) _____ . Paying attention to what goes on around you in the office helps you 3) _____ . If you make a mistake, just say that 4) _____ . If you stay late after work, your colleagues and boss will know that you are committed to your work and the company.

Text B

Pre-reading Task: Answer the following questions before reading the text.

1. What should you pay attention to when you start a new job?

2. In your opinion, what mistakes people might make when starting a new job?

3. How could we avoid the mistakes we make when starting a new job?

The Mistakes You Can Make When You Start a New Job

There are lots of mistakes you can make in a new job—showing up late on your first day, making personal phone calls all day, and wearing a tutu.

The worst thing you can do, and it's a mistake a lot of people do out of enthusiasm, is to storm into a new workplace and start making suggestions for improvement.

Here's an unrelated story to explain: A couple of years ago I was at a party at which I was to meet the new girlfriend of a dear friend of mine. This woman happened to be a hairstylist, who for some reason, was eager to make a good impression on me. About five minutes into the evening, she pointed at me and said, "I can fix that." I must have looked perplexed because then she said, "Your hair. I can fix it." I'm not sure how words like that could be received any way but poorly. I just said I was not aware my hair was broken.

So, now I'm not saying you're going to charge into the CIO's[1] office and tell him his hair is all wrong. But criticizing (which is what you're doing by offering a "better" way) a business process that has long been in place can feel like the same thing.[2] You cannot expect someone, even an employer, to be gracious when told indirectly that they've been doing things all wrong.

This is not to say that the time will not come for your insights. It will. But it's more important to learn the lay of the prevailing land before you presume to suggest changes.[3] It's also important that you prove yourself first so that others will take your suggestions more seriously.

Don't let your enthusiasm take over when starting a new job. Let's find out other mistakes you should avoid in order to get off on the right foot.

If you've finally managed to land a new job, don't get too excited. Your biggest challenge is yet to come, with experts warning the first 90 days will make or break your success in the job. Career expert Russell Johnson says the biggest mistake people make when they start in a new workplace is they don't realize how important the first three months actually are. "The first day is the most important day, first week is the most important week, and by the time the first 90 days are over you're either in or **you're toast**," said Mr. Johnson, managing director of EPR Career Management. "It's simply that people are making their impression and first impressions are so difficult to change."

Mr. Johnson says another major mistake people often make is they have too much confidence and don't ask for enough help. "If you ask for help you're basically **acknowledging** 'I'm a newcomer here and there's a lot I don't understand'," he said. Mr. Johnson said by asking for assistance you will learn more and you will create relationships with your colleagues. "People like people who don't think they know it all—everyone likes to be respected and the fact that you asked them **indicates** respect,"[4] he said.

Mr. Johnson said relationships will make or break your career—but some people make the mistake of being **dragged into gossip** in an effort to fit in. "Don't focus too much on relationships with colleagues," he said. "Be a bit independent of the good and bad opinions and get a **reputation** of someone who plays it straight."[5]

Another major mistake people make is they don't speak up when their new job is different from what they were promised, says Mike Roddy from recruitment firm Randstad. Mr. Roddy said you should not feel too nervous to **bring** it **up** with your boss, because the employer has made an investment by hiring you and it is in their interests to make sure you stay. "It's important that you don't sit on it and **simmer**—ask what's **reasonable** to change about the role because the job that you're doing is very different to what (the boss) said it would be,"[6] he said.

Nick Deligiannis, managing director of recruitment firm Hays, says new staff members often make the mistake of being too **forthright** with their opinions. "It's not a problem to have an opinion straight away, but don't be afraid to sit back and understand the **issues** in the business before you try to make an impact," he said. "**Assess** the personalities and **strengths** of your colleagues before **weighing in**." (761 words)

be toast（非正式）完蛋了，倒霉了

acknowledge v. 承认

indicate v. 指示；表明

drag into 硬把……拉扯进
gossip n. 流言蜚语；闲话

reputation n. 声誉，名声

bring up 提出；养育

simmer v. 即将爆发；内心充满
reasonable adj. 合理的

forthright adj. 直率的；坦白的
issue n. 事情；问题
assess v. 评估
strength n. 长处
weigh in 参与；发表评论

Notes

1. CIO=Chief Information Officer 首席信息官
2. *But criticizing (which is what you're doing by offering a "better" way) a business process that has*

long been in place can feel like the same thing. 然而批评（即你现在使用"较委婉"的方式做的事情）一个长期以来正常运转的工作流程也会给人带来同感。

括号中的部分是定语从句，解释说明了 criticizing 在此处的含义。所谓 a "better" way 也就是下文所讲的 when told indirectly that they've been doing things all wrong，即通过间接方式告诉对方所做的事情是错的。the same thing 是说就像上文"告诉首席信息官他的发型不合适"这件事一样，对一个长期以来正常运转的工作流程横加指责也会使人觉得不舒服。

3. *But it's more important to learn the lay of the prevailing land before you presume to suggest changes.* 但是在你贸然提出改变的建议之前，更重要的是了解现行的局面。

这句话中的 lay 是名词，意思为"位置；状态"；land 意思相当于 situation。the lay of the prevailing land 即 the present situation。

4. *People like people who don't think they know it all—everyone likes to be respected and the fact that you asked them indicates respect...* 人们都不喜欢那些认为自己无所不能的人——每个人都希望得到尊重，而你问他们问题则体现出了这种尊重……

know it all 意为"无所不知，博学多闻"。在 the fact that you... 中，that 引导的是同位语从句。

5. *Be a bit independent of the good and bad opinions and get a reputation of someone who plays it straight.* 对好的和不好的看法要有一些独立的判断，这样才能赢得为人诚实的声望。

Be a bit... bad opinions 是祈使句，后接 and 引导的句子表示结果，而祈使句则暗示某种条件。who plays it straight 作为 someone 的定语。

independent of (someone/something) 意为"不依赖……；独立于……"。如：The two departments are independent of each other. 这两个部门彼此独立。

play it straight 源自于习语 play straight (with someone): be honest and fair in one's dealings (with someone) 意为"诚实而公平；老实无欺"。

6. *It's important that you don't sit on it and simmer—ask what's reasonable to change about the role because the job that you're doing is very different to what (the boss) said it would be...* 重要的是不要把问题搁置起来，自己生闷气。因为你正做的工作和原来老板描述的情况大相径庭，所以你需要询问一下，对于你的职位能做哪些合理的改变……

sit on it 中的 it 指代本段开头提到的发现新工作与原来承诺的不符这件事情，即 that your new job is different from what you were promised. sit on: to delay dealing with something 搁置。

破折号起解释说明的作用，其后面的 ask... it would be... 是对其前面的 don't sit on it and simmer 的具体阐释，并且这两个动词短语共用一个主语 you，都包含在 It's important that... 引导的从句里。

Reading Comprehension

Decide whether the following statements are true (T) or false (F) according to the text.

(   ) 1. The worst thing you can do when starting a new job is wearing a tutu.

(   ) 2. The hairstylist at the party made a good impression on me by saying that she could fix my hair.

(   ) 3. If you know the business of the company clearly, others will take your advice on making changes.

(　　) 4. After starting a new job, the first three months are the important months to you.

(　　) 5. Even if your new job is different from what you were promised, you should not bring it up with your boss.

Vocabulary

Fill in the blanks with the given words or expressions. Change the form where necessary.

1. Peter _____ the office and shouted at the manager. (storm into)
2. The President's political advisers also _____ on the plan. (weigh in)
3. Ron does nothing but _____ and complain all the time. (criticize)
4. I will be angry if he _____ to question my judgment. (presume)
5. He _____ three new issues at the meeting. (bring up)
6. The study _____ a connection between poverty and crime. (indicate)
7. This report is _____ the impact of advertising on children. (assess)
8. The government must _____ what is happening and do something about it. (acknowledge)

Section C / Extending Your English

I. Approaching the reading skill: understanding stated information（理解明确表达的信息）1

阅读是理解语篇及获取、加工、处理信息的综合过程；是一个积极主动的思考、理解和接受信息的过程。在阅读过程中，最基本的技能是要正确理解文章中字面上明确表达的信息（stated information），即主要事实、特定信息或有关细节。一般说来，为了阐明文章的中心意思，作者总是运用大量的事实和细节来说明中心意思并进行各种不同的陈述，也就是说文章中的每一句话都是围绕主题而展开的，或是提供例证，或是进行分类比较，或是说明因果关系等。正确分析文章中的每个句子如何说明和解析中心意思，是提高阅读理解水平的关键。

下面通过一些例句来看一下明确表达的信息（stated information）在文章中如何体现。加下划线的文字为主题，加粗的文字为表明事实和细节的地方：

1. <u>It will be a busy day</u>. You will most likely **meet with the human resources department to complete paperwork, get settled into your workplace, establish computer passwords and much more**.

（第二句提供了一些例子，用以证明第一句中的主题"繁忙的一天"）

2. <u>Marketing decisions generally fall into four controllable categories</u>. These four categories (also known as the marketing mix) are **product, price, place** and **promotion**.

（第二句说明了营销决策的四个类别，围绕主题句进行了分类）

3. If you've finally managed to land a new job, <u>don't get too excited</u>. **Your biggest challenge is**

yet to come, with experts warning the first 90 days will make or break your success in the job.

（第二句中的事实作为原因解释了为什么"不能兴奋得过了头"这一主题）

通过上面对于文章中明确表达的信息的分析可以看出在通读全文、初步掌握文章大意的基础上，获得的信息越详细，理解的事实和细节越正确且越多，就越能深刻地理解文章的中心思想。

II. Applying the reading skill

Read the following passage and fill in the blanks with the given sentences as options.

Remember Your Very First Day of Work?

I'm working for a brand-**strategy** agency called The Brand Union, which does everything from advertising to brand design.¹ I am very happy to be able to work here for the following reasons. Firstly, I've got a chance of researching on the **packaging** design of hair care products produced by a client's competitors. Secondly, 1) _____.

But I wasn't this positive on my first day of work.² My first day was **absolutely terrifying**.

I ran into the office nervously and my heart was **pounding**. I tried to calm myself by **crossing my fingers** and hoping for some easy tasks that anyone could do. 2) _____ I hoped for anything but actual work—I was afraid that I'd prove to be the most **incompetent** fool in the workplace.

Things took a turn for the worse when I meet the other **intern**. Catherine is a second year MBA candidate who did her **undergraduate** studies at Stanford and worked for several companies before **pursuing** her master's. 3) _____ .What had I just signed up for?

We were introduced to our new **supervisors**, who briefed us on the projects we'd be working on for the month and their expectations of us. Throughout the meetings, Catherine was completely **at ease**. 4) _____ .

I went home after the first day feeling rather defeated. 5) _____. However, I still dragged my **butt** off to work the next day.³ And I found that the second day wasn't all that terrible. Neither was the third day. Or the fourth. And Friday was actually kind of fun.

---

strategy n. 策略

packaging n. 包装

absolutely adv. 绝对地，完全地
terrifying adj. 恐怖的
pound v. 剧烈跳动
cross one's finger 两指交叉以求好运
incompetent adj. 不能胜任的

intern n. 实习生
undergraduate n. 大学生
pursue v. 继续进行

supervisor n. 监督人，管理人

at ease 不拘束，自在

butt n. （口语）屁股

It's been a week and a half since I first **set foot** in the office, and I've been happily working away at my desk since. For someone who **started off** knowing nothing about the industry, I'm **getting along** just well. I can't wait to see where the next three weeks take me.[4]

(383 words)

set foot 踏上；涉足

start off 开始

get along 进展

Notes

1. *I'm working for a brand-strategy agency called The Brand Union, which does everything from advertising to brand design.* 我在一家叫做"扬特品牌同盟"的品牌策略机构工作。这家公司涉足从广告宣传到品牌设计的各种业务。

    The Brand Union 扬特品牌同盟，原扬特品牌咨询公司（Enterprise IG），是全球领先的品牌策略与识别形象咨询公司，提供从调研到战略、设计、联结以及评估在内的全方位品牌服务。公司创立于1976年，随后加入WPP集团，成为其子公司。

2. *But I wasn't this positive on my first day of work.* 但是我在工作的第一天可没有这么积极。

    this 在这里为程度副词，意思是"这么，这样地"，相当于 so。

3. *However, I still dragged my butt off to work the next day.* 然而我第二天仍然强打精神去上班。

    drag one's butt off 字面意思是"拖动屁股"，引申含义是强迫自己做本不愿意做的事情。butt（口语）屁股，与其相关的其他习惯用语还有：work one's butt off（很努力地做一件事）；freeze one's butt off（冷得把屁股冻僵）等。

4. *I can't wait to see where the next three weeks take me.* 我迫不及待地想知道接下来的三个星期我将表现如何。

    can't wait to do something 迫不及待地做某事。本句中 where the next three weeks take me 是动词 see 的宾语从句。

Options:

A. I'm learning a lot here, and everyone seems pretty eager to help out the youngest guy in the office.

B. Maybe I'd fetch them coffee and fax papers? Maybe they'd pretend I wasn't even there?

C. I am a sophomore majoring in Architecture and ten years her junior.

D. I smiled with the occasional head nod, mostly shutting up like a well-mannered child at the dinner table.

E. I felt a bit overwhelmed and was afraid of the road that lay ahead.

Section D / Self-evaluation

After learning this unit, I have grasped

Items	100%	80%	60%	Below 50%
Words				
Grammar				
Reading				

Notes to this unit:

Unit 4

On-the-Job Training

Learning Objectives

In this unit, you will learn

- to understand the importance of on-the-job training;
- to get basic information about on-the-job training;
- to master the new words and expressions related to no-the-job training;
- to apply the reading skill—understanding stated information.

Section A / Lead-in

I. For what jobs is the following training used?

Directions: Match the words or expressions in the box with the pictures.

(1)

(2)

(3)

(4)

(5)

(6)

> A. construction work   B. medical work   C. office work
> D. cookery   E. manufacturing   F. retail sales

II. Describe the above pictures.

Directions: Work in pairs to describe how training is used in these jobs (What does the trainer do? What do the trainees do?).

Section B / Embracing English

Text A

Pre-reading Task: Answer the following questions before reading the text.

1. Have you received certain trainings before? If so, what trainings?

2. In your opinion, what is workplace training?

3. How do you think of the importance of workplace training?

Why Is Workplace Training Important?

All employees require some degree of workplace training. The most experienced executive requires **briefings** to bring her up to speed on a company's financials, strengths, weaknesses and major competitors. **Entry-level** employees who have positions in **manufacturing** and quality control require **substantial** training time to learn the appropriate skills and processes **mandated** by the company. Software training is another **consideration**. Recent college graduates who are new to corporate America also require training and **mentoring** to help them learn their jobs and **assimilate** into the company culture.

Excellent training helps to reduce, and even **eliminate**, **costly** mistakes and errors in the workplace. Employees learn to master the basics of their jobs with the help of effective training and practice. Trainers model and **demonstrate** correct practices, showing employees the proper way to complete assignments. Testing and **certification validate** that the employee is competent in performing the assigned duties.[1] Confidence increases as training **instills** a sense of **accomplishment** in trainees and errors decrease with each training class.

Profits rise when everyone is trained properly. Sales increase when your sales team uses a solid selling model and is properly educated on its use. Quality improves when everyone understands his role in producing quality products. **Turnover** decreases when supervisors and managers receive training on management and hiring skills. Education about labor laws, **harassment** training and equal employment opportunity eliminate problems before they happen. The best training is **proactive** and continued **refresher** workshops keep your employees prepared for whatever changes come your way.[2]

With every training course your company culture is further defined. Practices, standards, procedures and methods are all defined when your employees attend training. History, **legends** and traditions pass from trainer to associate in well designed training courses. Your company is defined for new employees during **orientation** training and **cemented** during **follow-up** courses.[3] **Slogans**, sayings and stories are **passed on** to new generations of associates during every class. An excellent training process will ensure success both now and in the future.

Potential employees are attracted to and want to stay with a company that has an outstanding training program. Your marketing department will be pleased to use a well-trained and experienced workforce as a tool to promote your company. Customers, clients and applicants are happy to hear about your professional training and education programs that retain good people. The competitor never likes to know that they are competing against a team of highly educated and motivated individuals who love to work for you.

Companies that have a reputation for providing job training and educational programs for their workforce are highly sought after by potential employees. New college graduates especially know the need for training and compete for positions in companies that offer them career growth by supplying training programs. Companies like Xerox Corporation **tout** their learning and development programs such as the Xerox Personal Development Program created by each employee and his manager.[4] This program is an assessment of employee skills **in relation to** the job, career goals and the creation of a development plan to prepare for promotion.

The cost of turnover can **eat away** at company profits. Companies gain employee loyalty by creating a culture where each worker feels valued and has the ability to receive training for job success and career growth. SAS[5], a software company headquartered in Cary, North Carolina, has an extremely low turnover rate. According to the 2011 Fortune 100 Best Companies to Work For Survey, the turnover metrics at SAS are reported at a mere 2 percent. The company CEO, Jim Goodnight, **attributes** the success of the company to a culture that cares about an employee's personal and professional growth.

Companies that recognize the benefit of job training and development incorporate the **philosophy** into their annual strategic plans. Creating an environment of **ongoing** learning helps all employees upgrade their skills and continually increase their value to the organization.

(642 words)

New Words and Expressions

briefing /ˈbriːfɪŋ/	n.	information or instructions that you get before you have to do something 简报
entry-level /ˈentriˌlevəl/	adj.	suitable for unskilled or inexperienced workers 入门级的
manufacture /ˌmænjʊˈfæktʃə/	v.	to use machines to make goods or materials, usually in large numbers or amounts 制造，加工
substantial /səbˈstænʃəl/	adj.	large in amount or number 数目大的；可观的
mandate /mænˈdeɪt/	v.	formal to tell someone that they must do a particular thing 命令，要求
consideration /kənˌsɪdəˈreɪʃən/	n.	correct or suitable for a particular time, situation, or purpose 体谅；考虑
mentor /ˈmentɔː/	v.	to give someone help and advice over a period of time, especially help and advice related to their job 为……出谋划策；指导
assimilate /əˈsɪmɪleɪt/	v.	to completely understand and begin to use new ideas, information etc. 理解；吸收
eliminate /ɪˈlɪmɪneɪt/	v.	to completely get rid of something that is unnecessary or unwanted 去除，排除
costly /ˈkɒstli/	adj.	very expensive, especially wasting a lot of money 昂贵的，费用大的
demonstrate /ˈdemənstreɪt/	v.	to show or prove something clearly 展示，说明
certification /ˌsətɪfɪˈkeɪʃən/	n.	an official document that says that someone is allowed to do a certain job, that something is of good quality etc. 证明，保证
validate /ˈvælɪdeɪt/	v.	formal to prove that something is true or correct, or to make a document or agreement officially and legally acceptable 使有效，确认

instill /ɪnˈstɪl/	v.	to teach someone to think, behave, or feel in a particular way over a period of time 灌输
accomplishment /əˈkʌmplɪʃmənt/	n.	something successful or impressive that is achieved after a lot of effort and hard work 成就，成绩
turnover /ˈtɜːnˌəʊvə/	n.	the rate at which people leave an organization and are replaced by others （人员的）流动率
harassment /ˈhærəsmənt/	n.	when someone behaves in an unpleasant or threatening way towards you 烦恼；骚扰
proactive /prəʊˈæktɪv/	adj.	making things happen or change rather than reacting to events 有前瞻性的；积极主动的
refresher /rɪˈfreʃə(r)/	n.	a training course, usually a short one, that teaches you about new developments in a particular subject or skill, especially one that you need for your job 补习课程
legend /ˈledʒənd/	n	an old, well-known story, often about brave people, adventures, or magical events 传说，传奇
orientation /ˌɔːriənˈteɪʃən/	n.	the type of activity or subject that a person or organization seems most interested in and gives most attention to 定方位，方向，倾向
cement /sɪˈment/	v.	to make a relationship between people, countries, or organizations firm and strong 接合，巩固
follow-up /ˈfɒləʊʌp/	n.	something that is done to make sure that earlier actions have been successful or effective 后续行动
slogan /ˈsləʊgən/	n.	a short phrase that is easy to remember and is used in advertisements, or by politicians, organizations etc 标语，口号
tout /taʊt/	v.	(especially BrE) to try to persuade people to buy goods or services you are offering 兜售，推销（商品或服务）；拉生意
attribute /əˈtrɪbjuːt/	v.	to believe or say that a situation or event is caused by something 归于，属于
philosophy /fɪˈlɒsəfi/	n.	the study of the nature and meaning of existence, truth, good and evil, etc. 哲学
ongoing /ˈɒnˌgəʊɪŋ/	adj.	continuing, or continuing to develop 前进的，进行的
pass on		传递
in relation to		有关
eat away		侵蚀；蚕食

Notes

1. *Testing and certification validate that the employee is competent in performing the assigned duties.* 考试和证书证明了雇员有能力完成委派给他们的任务。

    testing 和 certification 分别指在职培训时对员工进行的考试和培训结束时颁发的证书。assigned 是过去分词作定语，表明它和 duties 之间有被动关系，即"被委派的任务"。

2. *The best training is proactive and continued refresher workshops keep your employees prepared for whatever changes come your way.* 最好的培训是具有前瞻性的，连续的补习课程可以使雇员为遇到的任何变化做好准备。

    whatever 在这里是形容词"无论怎样的"，除此之外，它还可以作代词"无论什么"。whatever 可以引导名词性从句，可视为 what 的强调说法，其含义大致相当于 anything that, no matter what...。whatever 在从句中可用作主语、宾语、定语。

3. *Your company is defined for new employees during orientation training and cemented during follow-up courses.* 通过定向培训，新雇员了解了公司；通过后续的课程，公司得到了巩固。

    orientation training 一般是对新员工的入职培训，培训内容包括公司的历史发展、各业务部门介绍、公司制度、薪酬福利体系、公司的战略计划等。

4. *Companies like Xerox Corporation tout their learning and development programs such as the Xerox Personal Development Program created by each employee and his manager.* 诸如施乐这样的公司推销他们的学习和发展项目，比如由员工和其经理参与的施乐个人发展项目。

    施乐公司（Xerox），是一家美国文案管理、处理技术公司，产品包括打印机、复印机、数字印刷设备以及相关的服务和耗材供应。

5. SAS，美国的商业智能软件供应商，全球最大的软件公司之一。

Reading Comprehension

I. Answer the following questions according to the text.

1. What kinds of people require workplace training?

2. What benefits can a company get from workplace training?

3. How does workplace training help employees?

4. What is Xerox Personal Development Program?

5. Why does SAS have an extremely low turnover rate?

II. Choose the best answer for each of the following questions according to the text.

1. What can employees learn from workplace training?
   A. The appropriate skills and processes mandated by their parents.
   B. Demonstration of mistakes and errors in the workplace.
   C. Basic knowledge of software.
   D. Testing and certification.

2. How does a company improve its quality of products?
   A. Sales team uses a solid selling model.
   B. Employees receive training on their roles in producing quality products.
   C. Supervisors and managers receive training on management and hiring skills.
   D. The company gives education about labor laws.

3. How to tell if a training is excellent or not?
   A. It ensures success both now and in the future.
   B. It defines the company.
   C. It has follow-up courses.
   D. It contains legends.

4. Which of the following companies will most likely be chosen by potential employees?
   A. A company that has marketing department.
   B. A company that has a well-trained and experienced workforce.
   C. A company that provides job training and educational programs.
   D. A company that creates the Xerox Personal Development Program.

5. What can you learn about SAS?
   A. It has an extremely high turnover rate.
   B. It is a software company headquartered in South Carolina.
   C. It is one of the 100 best companies in the world.
   D. It provides training for employees' career growth.

Vocabulary and Structures

I. Find the definition in Column B that matches the words in Column A.

Column A	Column B
1. briefing	A. information or instructions that you get before you have to do something
2. manufacture	B. to use machines to make goods or materials, usually in large numbers or amounts
3. assimilate	C. to completely understand and begin to use new ideas, information etc.
4. costly	D. very expensive, especially wasting a lot of money

5. turnover   E. the amount of business done during a particular period

6. orientation   F. the type of activity or subject that a person or organization seems most interested in and gives most attention to

7. attribute   G. to believe or say that a situation or event is caused by something

8. ongoing   H. continuing, or continuing to develop

II. Make the best choice to fill in the blanks with the given options in the box.

A. profit will rise, sales will increase, quality will improve and turnover will decrease

B. reduce or eliminate costly mistakes and errors in the workplace

C. companies provide job training and educational programs

D. require substantial training time to learn the appropriate skills and processes mandated by the company

E. the company culture is further defined during training

All employees, including the most experienced executive, entry-level employees and recent college graduates, require some degree of workplace training. Excellent training helps them learn the basics of their jobs and 1) _____ . For a company, if every employee is trained properly, 2) _____ . For new employees, 3) _____ . Potential employees will be attracted if 4) _____ . Creating an environment of ongoing learning helps all employees upgrade their skills and continually increase their value to the organization.

Text B

Pre-reading Task: Answer the following questions before reading the text.

1. How do you define the word "coaching"?

2. In your opinion, are coaching and training the same or different?

3. What might employee coaching involve?

Employee Coaching: When to Step In

A lot has been written about why managers should coach employees. A lot also has been written on how to coach employees. Very few articles help you know when to coach employees. That's what this article does.¹

Employee coaching involves helping employees **identify** solutions to their performance **barriers**. You are not coaching your employees when you tell them what to do.

Before you can effectively coach employees you must know that they are properly trained and that they know what is expected of them. These are the times to NOT coach employees.

Firstly, when an employee has not been completely trained it is a waste of your time and theirs to try to coach them in those **aspects** of their job. If they have been properly trained in part of their job, you can coach them in that part, but not in the areas where they have not yet been trained. Do the training first. Then do the employee coaching.

Secondly, it is pointless to coach employees who don't know what is expected of them and know how that is **measured**.² Remember that employee coaching is designed to help them **overcome** performance barriers. If they don't know what performance is expected of them they won't know how to get there. Set clear objectives for your employees. Then do the employee coaching.

Thirdly, when you are **in a hurry**, you will not do a good job. You will not take the time to help them identify solutions, but will be more likely to just tell them what to do. Make time to do it right.³ Then do the employee coaching.

Fourthly, when you are upset, you won't **exhibit** the enthusiasm and friendliness you need to be effective as an employee coach. You may not be fair or **equitable**. You may give even **subtle** signals to the employee that could undermine the coaching you have been doing up to this point. Get your emotions in check. Then do the employee coaching.

Other times, a good manager must step in and coach.

We need to let people make their own mistakes so they can learn from them. We can train them and advise them, which will help some of the time, but actual experience is often the best teacher. A good manager, therefore, will **hang back** and **resist** the **impulse** to jump in every time an employee **encounters** difficulty. A good manager will always monitor what their employees are doing, but will not intervene to coach their employees except in the following **circumstances**.⁴

When an employee is doing something that could cause harm to themselves or someone else, you have to step in. This is one instance where you can't let someone "learn from their mistakes".

---

identify v. 识别，鉴定
barrier n. 障碍

aspect n. 方面

measure v. 测量；估量
overcome v. 战胜，克服

in a hurry 匆忙

exhibit v. 展现

equitable adj. 公平的，公正的
subtle adj. 微妙的；隐约的

hang back 却步，犹豫
resist v. 忍耐，忍住
impulse n. 冲动
encounter v. 遇见
circumstance n. 状况

You need to provide coaching. Rather than tell them the solution, suggest a couple of **alternatives** and let the employee **figure out** which is best. Make sure they understand why the behavior they were planning is inappropriate.

You can't allow employees to do things that are **illegal** and you shouldn't allow them to do anything **unethical**. Whether their planned behavior is illegal/unethical because of intent or ignorance, you can't allow it. As with dangerous behaviors, provide alternatives, let them decide, and explain why the planned behavior was a poor choice.

You need your employees to work together as a team. If one member of the team is doing something that will cause the others to **exclude** him or her from the team, you have to step in. If an employee always **takes credit** for the team's work, you need to coach them. If an employee in a close area, like **cubicles**, always **yells** into the phone and disturbs those around him, you have to step in and help him find a different behavior.

When employees have repeatedly tried to solve a problem, and their solution isn't going to work, you need to step in. Often we try something and it fails. We try it again to make sure we did it the way we meant to and it still fails. If they keep trying, they aren't learning and you need to coach them.

Almost any mistake is going to cost the company money, either directly or in lost profits.[5] You can't step in every time an employee might make a mistake just to save money. Consider it an investment in the employee's learning and development. However, if their planned action would have a **significant** negative effect on the company financially, you have to step in. You have a responsibility to the company to protect its **fiscal** assets that is as great as the responsibility to develop its human assets. Provide the employee with alternative behaviors, let them figure out the appropriate choice, and explain why you had to step in. (800 words)

alternative *n.* 选择；供选择的东西
figure out 理解；想出
illegal *adj.* 违法的
unethical *adj.* 不道德的

exclude *v.* 排除
take credit 居功
cubicle *n.* （大房间中隔出的）小室
yell *v.* 大叫；叫着说

significant *adj.* 重要的，有含义的
fiscal *adj.* 财政的；会计的

Notes

1. *Very few articles help you know when to coach employees. That's what this article does.* 几乎没有文章帮你了解应该在什么时候指导员工。而本文正是关于这一主题。
   　　第二句的主语 that 指代前句中的 when to coach employees；does 是省略的说法，代替了前一句中的谓语动词，相当于 helps you know，所以第二句可以理解为 When to coach employees is what this article helps you know 或 This article helps you know when to coach employees。

2. *Secondly, it is pointless to coach employees who don't know what is expected of them and know how that is measured.* 第二点，如果员工不清楚公司对他们的期望是什么，也不知道公司如何来考察对他们的期望是否达标，那么指导员工就毫无意义。

know how that is measured 与前面的 know what is expected of them 共用一个 don't，所以在 who 引导的定语从句中这两个并列的动词短语都是否定的含义。上述两个动词短语中又分别包含由 how 和 what 引导的名词性从句，分别作两个 know 的宾语。

3. *Make time to do it right.* 腾出时间来把事情处理好。

make time 即 find time，意思为 "找时间，腾出时间，抽空"。形容词 right 作动词 do 的补语，用来补充说明 do 后的宾语 it 的性状或变化情况。

4. *A good manager will always monitor what their employees are doing, but will not intervene to coach their employees except in the following circumstances.* 优秀的经理总在员工工作的时候监控，而不会去插手指点，但下面的情况例外。

名词 circumstance 当 "事件，状况" 讲时常用复数形式，前面可加介词 in 或 under，表示 "在……情况下"。

5. *Almost any mistake is going to cost the company money, either directly or in lost profits.* 几乎任何错误都会造成公司金钱上的损失，或者是直接的，或者是利润受损。

cost the company money 意思为 make the company lose money。either directly or in lost profits 作动词 cost 的状语，说明金钱损失的方式。

Reading Comprehension

Decide whether the following statements are true (T) or false (F) according to the text.

(　　) 1. You must know your employees well before you can effectively coach them.

(　　) 2. You should coach employees in the part where they have not yet been trained.

(　　) 3. Your emotions might affect the employee coaching.

(　　) 4. A good manager will never intervene to coach their employees no matter what mistakes they make.

(　　) 5. You needn't step in when your employees have kept trying something but kept failing because they learn a lot from their failure.

Vocabulary

Fill in the blanks with the given words or expressions. Change the form where necessary.

1. They _____ as Americans at the airport. (identify)

2. Doctors say it is too early _____ the effectiveness of the drug. (measure)

3. Her financial problems could no longer be _____ . (overcome)

4. She _____ the temptation to laugh. (resist)

5. The crowd are on their feet _____ . (yell)

6. I first _____ him when studying at Cambridge. (encounter)

7. Alcoholism affects all _____ of family life. (aspect)

8. I think she may _____ what works for her so far. (figure out)

Section C / Extending Your English

I. Approaching the reading skill: understanding stated information（理解明确表达的信息）2

在上一单元中我们了解了什么是文章中明确表达的信息（stated information），介绍了不同的表达方式，如提供例证、进行分类比较、说明因果关系等，并且通过一些例句分析了明确表达的信息在文章中如何体现。在本单元中我们将从应试的角度来具体分析怎样把理解明确表达的信息这一阅读技巧应用于考试。在阅读理解题中，大多数问题是测试应试者对明确表达的事实和细节情况的理解。在做此类试题时，我们应从英语文章内容的一般组织方法上去考虑。分析事实和细节内容的有效方法是：在阅读过程中首先找出主题句（文章的中心意思往往通过主题句表现出来），然后分析其他各个句子与主题句的意义关系。这样我们可以清楚地掌握文章中的细节内容，找出问题的答案。下面举一个例子来说明：

During the American War of Independence, women were involved in the active fighting in three ways. First, as members of a distinct branch of the Continental Army, referred to as "Women of the Army", women staffed field hospitals and acted as a military support in such roles as water carriers. In an emergency, women water carriers, who had plenty of opportunities to observe the firing of cannons, could replace a wounded comrade. The second way that women were involved in the active fighting was as regular troop members who were in men's uniforms and fought side by side with their male counterparts. Theoretically, women were not supposed to be recruited into the army, but if a woman was a good soldier, no one made an issue of sex at a time when the army was so short of soldiers that boys not yet in their teens were also being recruited in violation of rules. Third, women were occasional fighters with local militia companies or committees of safety formed to protect the local community.

1) What is the main idea expressed in this passage?

   A. Women played an important role in military hospitals during the war.

   B. The Continental Army was successful in teaching women to fire cannons.

   C. The service of women in combat during the war.

   D. Women were active in com bat during the American War of Independence.

2) Women sometimes fired cannons because _____ .

   A. they had observed the procedure and could therefore substitute for disabled men

   B. local militia companies had trained them very carefully for emergency fighting

   C. they had a better safety record than men for using weapons

   D. it was against the law for young boys to fire weapons

3) What is probably the main reason that women were permitted to fight in the war even though their formal participation was discouraged?

　　A. Only women were successful as water carriers.

　　B. They were needed to make battle uniforms.

　　C. Colonial women were particularly healthy and strong.

　　D. The army desperately needed combat soldiers.

4) Women were involved in fighting the war for American independence in all of the following ways except as _____ .

　　A. members of committees of safety

　　B. support personnel at medical facilities

　　C. recruiters of soldiers for the Continental Army

　　D. combat troops in the regular army

　　本文的中心意思是：在美国独立战争中，妇女是如何积极参战的。文章中的每一句话都是围绕这一中心意思展开的。问题1)～4)的答案分别为D，A，D，C。第1)题问的是文章的中心意思，其余几题问的都是事实和细节内容，但后面几题的答案与第1)题是密切相关的。

　　在做阅读理解题时，找出文章的中心意思，理解每句话与中心意思的关系，确定题目的测试类型，对照题目和文章中的相关内容仔细阅读判别是理解文章中明确表达的事实和细节的重要方法。

II. Applying the reading skill

Read the following passage and choose the best answer to each of the following questions after your reading.

On-the-job Training

To grab the high-paid jobs of the future, workers will need the right skills. But given the **pace** of technological change, those skills are likely to have short **shelf lives**.[1] Results: a huge need for on-the-job training. Some companies, such as Xerox, already invest heavily in training programs. But if the economic **prophets** are correct, and long-term job security will soon be a **fading** memory, those efforts may not **make** much business **sense**. Why spend millions of dollars training workers you may not need next year — or even next month? Why not recruit skilled employees away from your competitors?

Economists call it the "free rider" problem. Because any one company can avoid the costs of paying for job training, it doesn't make sense for any company to pay for it. Unless that **trap** can be avoided, some **analysts** warn, employees won't get trained and crucial skills will remain **in short supply**.[2] "We want to build skills, but it's not good to have a situation where there is going to be a lot of

pace *n.* 速度，步调

shelf life 货架期，保质期

prophet *n.* 预言者，先知

fade *v.* 凋谢；消失

make sense 有意义

economist *n.* 经济学家

trap *n.* 陷阱；圈套

analyst *n.* 分析师

in short supply 供不应求

turnover," says Dupont's³ Korl.

But that particular problem may not be as **severe** as analysts' fear. Some corporations are **wrestling** with the job-training issue with surprising results.

Xerox is **emerging** as a leader in the field and now offers more than 120 training courses. The fastest-growing sector: courses for **high-end** computer professionals, such as system designers and network administrators. "There are $20-and $30-and $40-an-hour jobs," says Mitchell Fromstein, CEO of Manpower.

Offering expensive training programs to temporary workers may not seem like a **shrewd** business decision, given the high employee turnover. But Fromstein says Manpower has learned to regard training as a two-way street: teach workers the skills they need, and they'll keep coming back for more.

"That doesn't mean that people never take our training and go **elsewhere** for more money," Fromstein says. "But because we can deliver training on a very cost-effective basis, we're still seeing a good return on our investment."

What role should government play? Federal job-training efforts have a spotty record. The 14-year-old Jobs Training Partnership Act, for example, has delivered only **modest** employment and **wage** gains for adults and virtually no benefits of youths, according to a study by the Urban Institute, a politically **moderate** research group.

Another approach: tax incentives. Congress passed a law allowing firms to provide tax-free **tuition** to employees for job-related training. The program proved popular, and analysts give it high marks, but Congress allowed the tax break to **expire** last year in a budget–cutting move.⁴

(422 words)

severe *adj.* 严厉的，剧烈的
wrestle *v.* 斗争

emerge *v.* 浮现

high-end *adj.* 高端的

shrewd *adj.* 精明的；敏锐的

elsewhere *adv.* 在别处

modest *adj.* 适度的；中等的
wage *n.* 薪水；工资
moderate *adj.* （通常指政治方面）不极端的，温和的
tuition *n.* 学费

expire *v.* 期满，终止

Notes

1. *But given the pace of technological change, those skills are likely to have short shelf lives.* 但是考虑到技术变革的速度，那些技能有可能很快就过时了。

    given 作介词有两种用法：（1）（表示原因）考虑到，taking something into account；（2）（表示假设）倘若，假定，if。

2. *Unless that trap can be avoided, some analysts warn, employees won't get trained and crucial skills will remain in short supply.* 一些分析师警告说，除非能够避开这个陷阱，否则员工得不到培训，关键技能岗位仍将供不应求。

    正常的语序应该是把 some analysts warn 置于句首，即 Some analysts warn unless that trap can be avoided employees won't... supply. 有时为了强调，可以把句中的某一部

分置于句首。

  unless（如果不；除非）和 if... not 的用法常常是相同的，比如：

  Follow the green signs unless you have goods to declare. (...if you haven't any goods to declare.) 未携须申报货物者，沿绿色标记通行。

  但 unless 不可用以指尚未发生的事情之结果，因而不可用于"假想的"条件句中。

  unless（并非 if... not）也常用以引出对刚说过的话要增加的补充。

3. Dupont 即 S.T. Dupont，法国都彭，是知名的奢侈品品牌，创立于1872年，产品包括男士服装、皮具、配饰、打火机、书写工具等，深受各国政要、皇室贵族及明星的爱戴。

4. *The program proved popular, and analysts give it high marks, but Congress allowed the tax break to expire last year in a budget–cutting move.* 计划非常受欢迎，分析师们也给予其很高的评价。但国会在去年削减预算的行动中终止了这项减税。

  give it high marks 相当于 make good comments on it。

  budget-cutting 是名词加分词构成的形容词。这一类别的形容词具体来说可分为名词＋现在分词与名词＋过去分词两类，后者与被修饰名词之间存在被动关系。

Exercise: Choose the best answer for each of the following questions according to the text.

1. What is said about the on-the-job training in the text?

  A. It will turns out to be a fading memory.

  B. It is the consequence of fast technological changes.

  C. It does not make much business sense.

  D. It is likely to have short shelf lives.

2. The "free rider" problem _____ .

  A. can avoid the costs of paying for job training

  B. traps the companies into costly job-training courses

  C. keeps employees away from job-training courses

  D. gets some corporations in a situation of turnover

3. On offering job training programs, some corporations fear that _____ .

  A. they will have more temporary workers

  B. they will have to face the free-rider problem

  C. training courses will produce no good results

  D. the employees to have been trained will leave them

4. So far as training delivery is concerned, Fromstein believes that _____ .

  A. it pays off to make the efforts

  B. it doesn't prove a shrewd business decision

  C. it brings about high employee turnover

  D. it keeps coming back for more

5. It is implied in the last two paragraphs that _____ .

  A. on-the-job training programs call for the support of the government

  B. federal efforts have played an important role in job training to employees

C. the tax break programs have proved to be effective with high marks

D. Jobs Training Partnership Act guarantees tax-free tuition for job-related training

Section D / Self-evaluation

After learning this unit, I have grasped

Items	100%	80%	60%	Below 50%
Words				
Grammar				
Reading				

Notes to this unit:

Unit 5

Phone Calls

Learning Objectives

In this unit, you will learn

- to understand ways of making effective business phone calls;
- to get basic information about business phone calls;
- to master the new words and expressions related to business phone call;
- to apply the reading skill—guessing unknown words.

Section A / Lead-in

I. Can you describe these pictures?

Directions: Match the words or expressions in the box with the pictures.

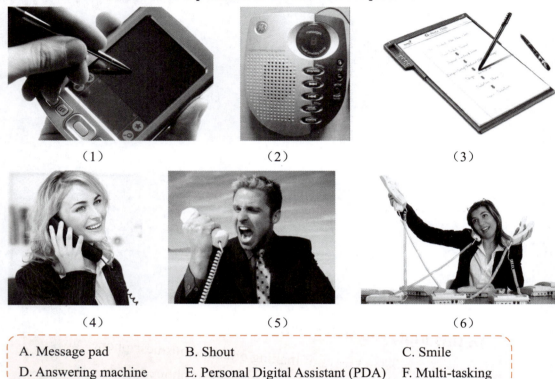

(1)　　　　　　　　　(2)　　　　　　　　　(3)

(4)　　　　　　　　　(5)　　　　　　　　　(6)

```
A. Message pad            B. Shout                         C. Smile
D. Answering machine      E. Personal Digital Assistant (PDA)   F. Multi-tasking
```

II. Describe the above pictures.

Directions: Work in pairs to talk about the tips for successful phone calls.

Section B / Embracing English

Text A

Pre-reading Task: Answer the following questions before reading the text.

1. How do you make successful business calls?

2. Is time management necessary when making calls?

3. What are the methods of telephone time management?

Time Management Tips for Outgoing Telephone Calls

Telephone time management is important because the telephone is still the primary communication tool for most small businesses. But much of the time that businesses spend using the telephone is a waste of time. **Instead of** communicating with the people we want to communicate with, we waste time talking to other people or machines. The following time management telephone tips will be of great use.

Whether they're suppliers, regular clients, or contractors, many of us call the same people repeatedly. Keep your information updated with time-saving details so you don't waste time. For instance, if I know that a particular person that I want to reach takes a lunch from 1 to 2 p.m. each day, I know not to waste my time trying to call her during this time.

Plan your **outgoing** telephone calls. Before you call, **jot** down the main goal of the goal and the key points you want to cover.[1] This will help you save time, **stick to** the point and cover everything you want to cover.

If you're calling someone who is entered into your contacts **database**, have all the information about the person you're calling in front of you when you call. Whether you're using a computer software program or PDA[2], this is a great memory help during the call and saves even more time. **Moreover**, if you want to make notes during a call (or do anything else while you're speaking on the telephone), a good **speakerphone** is **essential**. Freeing your hands can free up a lot of time.[3]

It's wise to leave a complete message when you do reach someone's answering machine or voice mail.[4] For example, "This is Susan Ward at (telephone number). I'm calling to discuss the **estimate for** product. You can reach me at (telephone number) this afternoon." Speaking your telephone number twice gives the **recipient** of the message a much better chance of getting it right and getting it written down without **replaying** the message.

When you're trying to reach someone and you haven't, you will call back—perhaps every half hour! But if you've left a proper message, there's no need to waste your time leaving repeated messages (and **filling up** the person's answering machine). Give the person you're calling a reasonable **amount** of time to call back, such as until the next business day.[5]

Schedule your telephone calls and try to make them all together in a single block of time.[6] Most of us aren't that good at **multi-tasking** and lose a great deal of **productivity** when we're **flipping back and forth** from one task to another.[7] So if you have a dozen calls to make in a particular day, it's more efficient to make them all in one hour than to make one or two, and then make another three calls an hour later, and another two 45 minutes after that.

Book your outgoing telephone calls, if possible. If it's not going to be a quick call, when you first call someone, introduce yourself, tell her why you're calling, and then ask her if it's a convenient time to talk or if she would prefer to book a time to discuss it. Then **arrange** that you will call her at that time. This can not only save you time **on the spot** but save time when you call the person back, because you'll both be prepared to discuss the issue.

If at all possible, make your outgoing telephone calls in "**prime** time[8]". Research has shown that more people are in their offices early in the morning and can be reached between 8 a.m. and 11 a.m.

(612 words)

New Words and Expressions

outgoing /ˈaʊtgəʊɪŋ/		*adj.*	going out or leaving a place 向外的
jot /dʒɒt/		*v.*	to write a short piece of information quickly 草草记下
database /ˈdeɪtəˌbeɪs/		*n.*	a large amount of data stored in a computer system so that you can find and use it easily 资料库；数据库
moreover /mɔːˈrəʊvə/		*adv.*	in addition 并且，此外
speakerphone /ˈspiːkəfəʊn/		*n.*	a telephone that contains a microphone and a loudspeaker, so that you can use it without holding it. Speakerphones are especially used in business meetings when groups of people in different places want to talk to each other 无绳电话，免提电话
essential /ɪˈsenʃl/		*adj.*	extremely important and necessary 必要的；本质的
estimate /ˈestɪmət/		*n.*	a calculation of the value, size, amount etc. of something 估价；评价
recipient /rɪˈsɪpɪənt/		*n.*	someone who receives something 接受者；收件人
replay /ˌriːˈpleɪ/		*v.*	to hear again; to show again 重放；重播
amount /əˈmaʊnt/		*n.*	a quantity of something such as time, money, or a substance 量；数量；数额；总数
schedule /ˈʃedjuːl/		*v.*	to plan that something will happen at a particular time 把……安排在；排定；预定
multi-tasking /mʌlti-ˈtɑːskɪŋ/		*adj.*	doing more than one thing at a time 同时处理多重任务的
productivity /ˌprɒdʌkˈtɪvəti/		*n.*	the rate at which goods are produced, and the amount produced, especially in relation to the work, time, and money needed to produce them 生产率，生产力
flip /flɪp/		*v.*	to move something with a quick sudden movement so that it is in a different position 急促转动，蹦跳
arrange /əˈreɪndʒ/		*v.*	to organize or make plans for something such as a meeting, party, or trip 安排，整理
prime /praɪm/		*adj.*	of the very best quality or kind 最好的；主要的
instead of			代替
stick to			忠于，信守
fill up			装满，填满
back and forth			来回地，往复地
on the spot			立刻；当场

Notes

1. *Before you call, jot down the main goal of the goal and the key points you want to cover.* 打电话前，快速写下主要目的和想说的关键点。

    jot down 意为"快速写下"。此句中的 you want to cover 是定语从句修饰名词 points。

2. PDA：掌上电脑。

3. *Freeing your hands can free up a lot of time.* 释放双手，能腾出大量时间。

    此句中 freeing your hands 为主语。

4. *It's wise to leave a complete message when you do reach someone's answering machine or voice mail.* 当你在电话答录机或语音信箱留言时，最好留下完整信息。

    it 为形式主语，真实主语为不定式短语 to leave a complete message。

5. *Give the person you're calling a reasonable amount of time to call back, such as until the next business day.* 给你通话的对方留足够的时间回复，比方说可等到下一个营业日。

    此句中 you're calling 为定语从句修饰 person。

6. *Schedule your telephone calls and try to make them all together in a single block of time.* 把电话集中在一个时间段拨打。

    此句是祈使句。a block of time 意为"一个时间段"。

7. *Most of us aren't that good at multi-tasking and lose a great deal of productivity when we're flipping back and forth from one task to another.* 我们大多数人不那么擅于同时处理多重任务，周旋于一项又一项任务时会大大降低工作效率。

    be good at 意为"擅于"，from to 意为"从……到"；that good，此处 that 为程度副词，表示"到那种程度"。当 that 用来表示程度的时候，一般都是用于疑问句或否定句中。

8. prime time：（广播电视）黄金时间。

Reading Comprehension

I. Answer the following questions according to the text.

1. Why do you need to update your information?

2. How to plan your outgoing phone calls?

3. What is the purpose of using a computer software program or PDA?

4. Is speakerphone useful when making a call?

5. Why does the author give an example in paragraph 5?

II. Choose the best answer for each of the following questions according to the text.

1. Why do you speak your telephone number twice when leaving a message?
   A. Because you have much time.
   B. Because the signal goes fuzzy.
   C. Because you want to leave a clear message.
   D. Because you gave a wrong number.

2. The word "block" in paragraph 7 probably means _____ .
   A. amount   B. street   C. building   D. obstacle

3. When you call someone for the first time, it is advisable to _____ .
   A. introduce yourself loudly and quickly
   B. introduce your family and education
   C. book a table to have a meal
   D. book a time to call again

4. When is the best time to make a business call?
   A. Morning.   B. Lunchtime.   C. Midnight.   D. Afternoon.

5. Which of the following statement can tell you how to save time?
   A. Do not write down main points.
   B. A full and complete message is always helpful.
   C. Quick and omitted answers save time.
   D. Make a call at any time you like.

Vocabulary and Structures

I. Find the definition in Column B that matches the words in Column A.

Column A	Column B
1. primary	A. to organize or make plans for something
2. moreover	B. a calculation of the value, size, amount etc. of something
3. arrange	C. in addition
4. jot	D. to plan that something will happen at a particular time
5. estimate	E. chief, most important
6. replay	F. a subject or problem
7. schedule	G. to hear again
8. issue	H. to write a short piece of information quickly

Phone Calls Unit 5

II. Make the best choice to fill in the blanks with the given options in the box.

> A. It is advisable for you to leave a full message
> B. keep the information of the person you are calling in front of you
> C. Try to book your call with the recipient
> D. A plan of your main points can help you stick to your purpose
> E. Update your information as soon as possible

Since much of time spent in making telephone is a waste of time, time management skills are of importance. 1) _____ if you do not want to waste time. 2) _____ when making calls. If you tend to save even more time, 3) _____ . 4) _____ when you reach an answering machine because it will give the recipient chances to have correct information. 5) _____ , which can not only make both of you prepared but save time.

Text B

Pre-reading Task: Answer the following questions before reading the text.

1. How can you effectively handle inbound phone calls?

2. How can you manage time when making an inbound call?

3. What is a proper phone greeting when making an inbound call?

Time Management Tips for Inbound Phone Calls

Inbound phone calls can **eat up** a lot of time and seriously **decrease** your productivity by **pulling** you **away** from other tasks.[1] But just as there are ways of handling outgoing phone calls that will improve your time management, there are ways of handling inbound phone calls to **cut down** on the amount of time you **burn up** speaking on the phone.

A proper phone greeting is a good beginning for business call. For example, when answering the phone say something such as, "Cypress **Technologies**. Susan speaking. May I help you?" This not only lets the caller know that they've reached a business, but puts the responsibility on him to answer the question, saving time on questions such as,[2] "Is this Cypress Technologies?", and **meaningless** chat.

Think and **prioritize** as you speak. Is the call best handled right

---

inbound *adj.* （电话）打进来的，呼入的
eat up 消耗，吃完
decrease *v.* 减少，减小
pull away 拉掉，扯掉
cut down 削减，缩短
burn up 消耗；烧毁

technology *n.* 技术，工艺
meaningless *adj.* 无意义的；无目的的
prioritize *v.* 把事情按优先顺序排好；优先处理；使优先

now or later? Many of the telephone calls businesses receive are quick questions that are easily answered, such as, "How late are you open?" But others involve more **complex** and **time-consuming** answers. If that's the case, tell the caller so, and ask when it would be convenient to call her back to discuss it.³

Use techniques such as **paraphrasing** and **summarizing** to keep phone calls on track. If you're speaking to someone who seems to want to chat or **wander** from the point, say something such as, "So what I hear you saying is..." or "So the key points are..." or "Is (**insert** summary) a fair summary of what you were saying?" It's hard to be chatty with someone who refuses to chat.

Get in the habit of closing each inbound phone call with a summary of whatever action you and the caller have agreed to take.⁴ While this will only take seconds in most cases, it can save you a lot of time by avoiding mistakes and the need to **double-check**. For example, after a conversation during which you arranged a meeting with a client, you might say, "Good. I'll meet with you at your office at (insert **location**) at 10 a.m. tomorrow and we'll **go over** the job together."

Keep a message **pad** and writing tools by all your phones, so you can write down details during the inbound phone call. This is not only good time management at the time, helping to keep you focused on the call, but a help to time management later if you need to find and/or review the details of a particular conversation.⁵

Give your clients and customers the email **option**. Many of them will use email to contact you **rather than** phoning if they know what your email address is.⁶ Ensure that your company's email address is clear on your business cards and on your website, if you have one. If you have their email addresses, send email to your **current** clients and customers, mentioning the email option and presenting it as a way to improve communications.

Use technology to manage the time you're spending answering the phone. As **a minimum**, your business should have an answering machine and voice mail. **Set** these **up** with **appropriate** business words, and use them to answer the telephone for you when you're out of the office or need to work on something **uninterrupted**. Then schedule time to answer these telephone messages each day. **In terms of** time management, you'll gain valuable time by grouping telephone calls together.

If you're running a home-based business, get a separate business

---

complex *adj.* 复杂的
time-consuming *adj.* 费时的

paraphrase *v.* 将……释义
summarize *v.* 总结
wander *v.* 离题；闲逛
insert *v.* 插（话等），插入

get in the habit of 养成习惯

double-check *v.* 将……仔细检查；复核
location *n.* 位置；场所
go over 察看

pad *n.* 便条纸簿

option *n.* 选择
rather than 而不是

current *adj.* 当前的，流行的

minimum *n.* 最低限度，最小量
set up 建立，建造
appropriate *adj.* 适当的，恰当的
uninterrupted *adj.* 不间断的，连续的
in terms of 就……而论；在……方面

phone or line. You need to have a second "business-only" telephone with its own "business-only" answering machine and/or voice mail. Not only is this more professional, but it will save you the time it takes to **go through** messages and determining which ones are business-related.[7]

go through 通过，经历

It's always best to have a person answer the phone. Having a machine to **pick up** or worse, an automated "choose one of these numbers" system is dangerous when people don't **bother** to leave messages or call back.[8] If answering inbound phone calls is **taking up** too much time during your day, consider hiring a **receptionist** or a professional answering service to answer the phone for you. Having someone else to answer the phone will increase your productivity and bring better sales.

pick up 接电话；拾起
bother v. 烦扰
take up 占用
receptionist n. 前台接待员

Keep a written **script** of frequently asked questions (and answers) posted by your phone. It saves you and your employees' time if they don't have to search for answers or think about how to answer a request when answering the phone.

script n.（演讲，戏剧，广播等的）脚本，底稿

The telephone is supposed to be a business tool, not a disturbing timewaster that rules your working day. Handling your inbound phone calls according to these time management tips will help you better manage your time, improve your productivity, and **put** your telephone **back** in its proper place—helping you run your business rather than running you.

(817 words)

put back 把……放回原处；拖延

Notes

1. *Inbound phone calls can eat up a lot of time and seriously decrease your productivity by pulling you away from other tasks.* 呼入电话会占用你大量时间，让你无法做其他工作，严重降低你的工作效率。

    此句中 by doing 表示通过某种方式，情态动词 can 表示可能性。

2. *This not only lets the caller know that they've reached a business, but puts the responsibility on him to answer the question, saving time on questions such as ...* 这不仅让来电者知道他们打入的是商业电话，还省去他们问一些问题的时间，转而直接回答问题。

    not only...but... 意为"不但……而且……"，又作 not only... but (also)... ，并列连词，在句中常用来连接两个对等的成分，also 可以省略。用来连接两个主语时，谓语动词的单、复数形式遵循"就近"原则，即和 but (also) 后的名词或代词的数一致。

3. *If that's the case, tell the caller so, and ask when it would be convenient to call her back to discuss it.* 如果问题复杂，回答耗费时间，告诉来电者将在适当时间回复她。

    If that's the case，联系上文，可知 the case 意为 If that involves more complex and time-consuming answers。

4. *Get in the habit of closing each inbound phone call with a summary of whatever action you and the caller have agreed to take.* 养成这样一个习惯，结束每一个呼入电话时总结你和来电者达成的共识。

  此祈使句中嵌套了一个定语从句，修饰和限定名词 action。由于先行词 action 在从句中是宾语，关系代词 that 被省略。

5. *This is not only good time management at the time, helping to keep you focused on the call, but a help to time management later if you need to find and/or review the details of a particular conversation.* 这不仅能帮你管控时间，专注谈话，还能帮你在日后回顾某段电话内容时节省时间。

  此长句中主要结构是 not only... but 连接的两个并列分句，第一个分句，helping 为现在分词作状语；第二个分句中包含了一个 if 引导的条件状语从句。

6. *Many of them will use email to contact you rather than phoning if they know what your email address is.* 如果他们中的许多人知道你的电子邮件地址，他们会用电子邮件而不是电话联系你。

  rather than "而不是"，用作并列连词，连接两个平行结构。既可以表示主观愿望上的抉择，意为"是……而不是……"或"与其……宁可……"，也可以表示客观程度上的差异，"与其说是……不如说是……"。它连接的并列成分可以是名词、代词、形容词、介词或介词短语、动名词、动词不定式短语等。

7. *Not only is this more professional, but it will save you the time it takes to go through messages and determining which ones are business-related.* 这不仅更专业，还会在你浏览并判断哪些是与业务相关信息时节省时间。

  在此句中，not only 放在句首时，后接句子要用倒装结构。

8. *Having a machine to pick up or worse, an automated "choose one of these numbers" system is dangerous when people don't bother to leave messages or call back.* 如果有人不愿留言或回电话，那么机器接电话或自动"选择按键"系统接电话则有风险。

  having 动名词结构是这个句子中的主语；而以 when 引导的从句为条件状语从句。

Reading Comprehension

Decide whether the following statements are true (T) or false (F) according to the text.

  ( ) 1. Complicated questions must be answered first.

  ( ) 2. You need to chat with the person who is away from the point.

  ( ) 3. It is suggested that you should make a summary of each inbound call.

  ( ) 4. Home phone should be used for your home-based business because it is economical.

  ( ) 5. Having a person to answer the phone can improve your efficiency.

Vocabulary

Fill in the blanks with the given words or expressions. Change the form where necessary.

  1. These customers were satisfied with the way their complaints were _____ . (handle)

2. All of us have the _____ to protect the environment. (responsibility)

3. You have to take the _____ of this issue into account. (complex)

4. He has _____ his views at the end of the report. (summarize)

5. They have several _____ to solve this problem. (option)

6. The _____ trend is towards casual clothing. (current)

7. It really _____ me that he'd forgotten my birthday. (bother)

8. Much of my time was _____ by the tough task. (take up)

Section C / Extending Your English

I. Approaching the reading skill: guessing unknown words （猜测生词词义）1

  在阅读理解中，你毫无疑问地会遇到生词。但是碰到生词就查词典不是好习惯，而且会分散阅读时的注意力。考试时也不允许查词典。那么如何渡过生词关？其实判断生词词义有一系列方法，如：比较和对比、单词结构和上下文逻辑关系等。

  在文章中，作者有时会运用一些相互对应、互为反义的词语，使不同事物的特点更为突出。我们可以透过两种事物或现象的对比描述，寻找文中相互对比、相互对照的线索，从其中一个熟悉的词反推出生词词义。例如：

  1. Most of us agreed, however, Bill dissented.

  从 however 这一转折词可推知，dissent 与 agree 的意思相反，意为"不同意"。

  2. Her voice was usually soft and sweet, but now it is hoarse.

  她现在的状况与过去相对比，过去她的声音是 soft and sweet，那么现在就是 hoarse（沙哑的）了。

  3. A good supervisor can recognize instantly the adept workers from the unskilled ones.

  根据句法结构可知 the adept workers 和 the unskilled ones 为对比关系，意义相反。由 the unskilled ones 可推出 the adept workers 为熟练工人。

  4. Someone liked milk, but others abhorred it.

  通过 but 一词我们知道 abhor 是 like 的反义词，like 的意思是"喜欢"，那么 abhor 就应该是"厌恶"的意思。

  阅读中还可运用合成、转化、派生等构词法知识来猜测词义。通过分析词缀及词根猜测单词含义。

  5. They overestimate the interviewer's ability and asked him many difficult questions.

  词缀 over 的意思为"过分"，而 estimate 意为"估计"，因此可推测 overestimate 意为"过高估计"。

  6. Take out all removable parts and wash them with warm water.

  removable 一词由词根 move+ 前缀 re+ 后缀 able 构成，可推知意为"可移动的，可拆装的"。

  在学习中要掌握一些常见的词缀及其含义。如：形容词后缀有 -ful, -less, -y, -ing, -able 等；名词后缀有 -or, -er, -tion, -ist, -th, -ment, -age, -ness 等；构成反义词的前缀有 un-, dis-, in-, im-, ir-, non- 等。有特定意义的词缀有 re-（重新，再），co-（合作的），anti-（反对的），over-（过

高的），micro-（微型的），fore-（超前的），inter-（国际的，相互的），pre-（先前的，提前的），super-（超级的），tele-（远）等。

在阅读中，根据上下文的语境暗示，运用逻辑推理来猜测生词词义也是经常用到的方法。

7. He is a resolute man. Once he sets up a goal, he will not give up easily.

once 引导的主从复合句里描述了"他"的个性：一旦树立目标，就不会放弃。因此可推出 resolute 应为"坚决的，有决心的"之意。

8. Ventilation, as you know, is a system or means of providing fresh air.

此句中 ventilation 可能是个生词，但 is 后面的部分是对该词的明确定义。是什么东西或什么手段才能提供新鲜空气呢？所以不难看出 ventilation 这个词的意思是"通风设备"。

结合下面例句，进一步说明如何理解生词。

1. His impudent behaviors were like that of a spoiled child.（比较法，介词 like 是关键词，like that of a spoiled child 这个短语的意思是"行为如同被宠坏的孩子一般"，由此推断，impudent 的意思应该为"无礼的"。）

2. I found the novel interesting, but my sister said it was tedious.（对比法，but 是关键词，表示转折，由 but 一词前面的形容词 interesting（有趣的）的词义，可以推测，tedious 意为乏味的。）

3. Overwork may cause many diseases.（词缀法，前缀 over 意为"过量的"，由此可推测 overwork 意为"工作过度"。）

4. The two philosophical theories were incompatible: one admitted the existence of free will: the other denied it.（上下文逻辑法，关键词为 one...（一种），the other...（另一种），incompatible 意为"不相容的，矛盾的"。）

判断生词词义的方法除了上文提到的之外还有其他很多种，平时在做阅读练习时，应该有意识地运用这些阅读技巧培养自己的猜词悟意能力。

II. Applying the reading skill

Read the following passage and choose the best answer to each of the questions after your reading.

How to Make a Good Impression on the Phone

The person who answers the telephone has huge power. He or she can help further the company's purposes or **hinder** them. Good telephone manners are of importance, especially for **sales-oriented** businesses that require an expanding customer base.[1] Potential customers may not be familiar with a company's products or services. In many cases, they will base their business decisions on their telephone contact with the organization. Current customers may be calling for more information about a product or to voice their questions.

Follow company **policy** when answering the telephone. For

hinder v. 阻碍，妨碍
sales-oriented adj. 销售型的，以销售为导向的

policy n. 政策，方针

example, people in accounting and law offices like to produce a solid image. An accountant or lawyer may instruct his or her assistant to answer the telephone, "Good morning, Paul Smith's office." On the other hand, marketing and computer **personnel** may decide to use a more casual tone and answer, "Welcome to the Omega Group. Hope you are having a wonderful day."

personnel *n.* 职员

Find out the customer's name and the purpose of his or her call within the first few minutes of the conversation. If the customer hesitates and **tends to** speak something meaningless, **take charge of** the conversation and **obtain** the necessary information. Use a notepad to write down key names and points. Whenever possible, take the customer's name down.

tend to 有……的倾向
take charge of 开始管理，接管
obtain *v.* 取得某物

Smile is a key to successful business call. Potential customers will respond favorably to a pleasant and cheerful voice. When speaking, **vary** the expression and tone and speak all words as clearly as possible. Do not, however, become too familiar and tell too many personal and company details. The call may be a long one, especially if English is not the person's first language. Listen carefully and do not interrupt the customer. Do not correct grammar or pronunciation. **At intervals**, restate what you think the customer has said and ask for further **clarification**.

vary *v.* 改变

at intervals 不时；到处
clarification *n.* 澄清，说明

Avoid putting callers on hold for a long period of time.[2] Potential customers may change their minds and call other businesses if they do not receive immediate attention. If you cannot deal with a caller's request, ask if you can call him or her later. Return the call before the end of the business day or first thing the next morning.[3]

Most customer inquiries involve a simple question or request. If company policy prevents you from taking any immediate action, tell the customer that you will talk to your supervisor on his or her behalf. Provide the customer with a timeline for follow-up **procedures**.

procedure *n.* 步骤，手续

(406 words)

Notes

1. *Good telephone manners are of importance, especially for sales-oriented businesses that require an expanding customer base.* 电话礼仪很重要，对于需要不断发展客户的销售型企业尤其如此。
   此句中 business 后 that 引导的为定语从句，进一步说明是哪类企业。
2. *Avoid putting callers on hold for a long period of time.* 不要长时间搁置呼叫者。
   此句为祈使句。动词 avoid 后跟动名词。
3. *Return the call before the end of the business day or first thing the next morning.* 下班前回电，或

是第二天一早回电。

并列连词 or 后面的分句里省略了 return the call；first thing the next morning 这个短语为时间状语，说明回电的时间。

Exercise: Read the text again and finish the following exercises. Choose the closest expression of each underlined word by using the above-mentioned reading skills.

1. He or she can help further the company's purposes or <u>hinder</u> them.
   A. use   B. stop   C. fulfill   D. conceal

2. People in accounting and law offices like to produce a <u>solid</u> image.
   A. serious   B. noble   C. informal   D. vivid

3. If the customer hesitates and tends to speak something <u>meaningless</u>, take charge of the conversation and obtain the necessary information.
   A. critical   B. unexpected   C. hopeless   D. unimportant

4. At intervals, <u>restate</u> what you think the customer has said and ask for further clarification.
   A. review... assumption   B. write... information
   C. retell... explanation   D. require... expression

5. If company policy prevents you from taking any immediate action, tell the customer that you will talk to your <u>supervisor</u> on his or her behalf.
   A. administrator   B. company   C. client   D. secretary

Section D / Self-evaluation

After learning this unit, I have grasped

Items	100%	80%	60%	Below 50%
Words				
Grammar				
Reading				

Notes to this unit:

Unit 6

Agenda

Learning Objectives

In this unit, you will learn

- to know what is an agenda;
- to create an agenda;
- to master the new words and expressions related to agenda;
- to apply the reading skill—guessing unknown words.

Section A / Lead-in

I. What does this column tell us?

Directions: Choose the proper expressions from the categories and fill in the form.

1	2	3	4
	8:00 – 9:00	Working Breakfast	Flora Cafe
18th Sept	9:00 – 10:00	Opening Ceremony	Exhibition Center
	10:00 – 11:30	Discussion	Conference Center
	11:30 – 12:00	Closing Statement	Conference Center

A. Date   B. Title   C. Time
D. Activity   E. Venue   F. Purposes

II. Describe the above column.

Directions: Work in pairs to talk about how to make an agenda.

_____

_____

Section B / Embracing English

Text A

Pre-reading Task: Answer the following questions before reading the text.

1. What is meeting agenda?

2. How do you make an agenda?

3. Why do you make an agenda before a meeting?

How to Structure an Agenda

A meeting **agenda** is the list of items that **attendees** hope to accomplish at a meeting. **In combination with** meeting **minutes,** the materials that **participants** receive after a meeting, the agenda is the plan for the meeting and the reported follow-up for the **prior** meeting.[1] A meeting agenda can help make every meeting productive.

Once a meeting has been decided on as the best communication method, an agenda is necessary. A meeting agenda ensures that the meeting will be a productive use of everyone's time. An agenda can focus the attendee's efforts and provide a structure to accomplish the meeting purpose. An effective agenda contains **defined outcomes**, **logistics** information for the meeting, attendee roles and responsibilities, a meeting time line and information needed for the meeting.[2]

Provide the **foundation** for the meeting's success by defining its purpose **along with** a set of **objectives** or desired outcomes. Meeting purposes include informing, persuading, selling, instructing, problem-solving and making a decision. The meeting purposes should support the meeting's outcomes. The first **item** on any meeting time line should be a **restatement** of the meeting purpose and desired outcomes. This restatement helps all attendees understand why they are in the meeting and what they are expected to accomplish.

Describe all essential pieces of meeting logistics information. Meeting logistics information includes the meeting date; time (including daylight saving time or international time **designations**); location, including login information for online meetings; and attendee list. It is important for meeting **facilitators** to hold a meeting in an appropriate setting that supports the work to be accomplished.[3] Online meeting attendees also need to know who to contact **in case** they experience technical problems.

Ensure that all people attending a meeting know what is expected of them during the meeting. At a minimum, the roles of meeting facilitator and note taker should be defined. Moreover, state the roles of any **presenters**. The agenda should make clear who **is responsible for** each **topic** and how each topic will **contribute to** the meeting outcomes.

Define a meeting time line that keeps the meeting moving forward and covers the topics necessary to achieve the meeting outcomes. A time line should be structured as **a series of** rows and **columns**, with each row **representing** a different topic. The columns should be the time **allocated** to the topic, a description of the topic, and the responsibility for facilitating or presenting the topic. The minimum topics required for any meeting are an introduction that restates the meeting purpose and desired outcomes, and a **conclusion** that may include the assignment of action items.

State what information will be covered during the meeting and what information attendees should review prior to attending the meeting.[4] The agenda should also state what information each attendee needs to bring to the meeting. **Distribute** the agenda prior to the meeting and include needed information as an **attachment**. The agenda should be distributed to participants several days **in advance of** a meeting, minimally 24 hours, so that participants have the opportunity to prepare for the meeting.[5] It is important for all attendees to have the latest information about the meeting on the agenda.

(523 words)

New Words and Expressions

agenda /ə'dʒendə/   *n.*   a list of the subjects to be discussed at a meeting 议程

attendee /ˌə͵ten'diː/   *n.*   someone who is at an event such as a meeting or a course 出席者；在场者

combination /ˌkɒmbɪ'neɪʃən/   *n.*   two or more different things that exist together or are used or put together 结合，联合

minutes /'mɪnɪts/   *n.*   an official written record of what is said and decided at a meeting 会议记录

participant /pɑː'tɪsɪpənt/   *n.*   someone who is taking part in an activity or event 参与者

prior /'praɪə/   *adj.*   existing or arranged before else or before the present situation, previous 在先的

define /dɪ'faɪn/   *v.*   to describe something correctly and thoroughly, and to say what standards, limits, qualities etc it has that make it different from other things 使明确，规定

outcome /'aʊtkʌm/   *n.*   the final result of a meeting, discussion, war etc - used especially when no one knows what it will be until it actually happens 结果；结局

logistics /lə'dʒɪstɪks/   *n.*   the practical arrangements that are needed in order to make a plan that involves a lot of people and equipment successful 物流；后勤；组织工作

foundation /faʊn'deɪʃən/   *n.*   principle, idea or fact on which sth is based; basis（作为某事的）基本原则，思想或事实；基础

objective /əb'dʒektɪv/   *n.*   something that you are trying hard to achieve, especially in business or politics 目标；目的

item /'aɪtəm/   *n.*   a single thing, especially one thing in a list, group, or set of things 项目，条款

restatement /riː'steɪtmənt/   *n.*   stating something again 重申

designation /ˌdezɪg'neɪʃən/   *n.*   the act of choosing someone or something for a particular purpose, or of giving them a particular description 任命；委派

facilitator /fə'sɪlɪteɪtə/   *n.*   someone who helps a group of people discuss things with each other or do something effectively 促进者

presenter /prɪ'zentə/   *n.*   someone who is at a meeting or propose something 出席者，提出者

topic /'tɒpɪk/   *n.*   a subject that people talk or write about 话题

series /'sɪəriːz/   *n.*   a number of things, events, etc. of a similar kind, esp. placed or occurring one after another 一系列的事物

column /ˈkɔləm/	n.	one of two or more vertical sections of printed material on a page 列，栏	
represent /ˌreprɪˈzent/	v.	stand for or be a symbol or equivalent of (somebody/something) 表示，代表	
allocate /ˈæləkeɪt/	v.	to use something for a particular purpose, give something to a particular person etc. especially after an official decision has been made 分配，分派	
conclusion /kənˈkluːʒən/	n.	the end or final part of something 结论，结尾	
distribute /dɪˈstrɪbjuːt/	v.	to share things among a group of people, especially in a planned way, give out 分发	
attachment /əˈtætʃmənt/	n.	a document or file that is sent with an email message 附件	
in combination with		与……结合（联合）	
along with		与……在一起	
in case		倘若，如果	
be responsible for		对……有责任	
contribute to		有助于；促成	
a series of		一系列	
in advance of		在……的前面	

Notes

1. *In combination with meeting minutes, the materials that participants receive after a meeting, the agenda is the plan for the meeting and the reported follow-up for the prior meeting.* 会议纪要是与会者通常在会后收到的文件材料，会议议程则是会议计划和上次会议的后续报告。

   the materials 为 meeting minutes 的同位语，that 引导的定语从句说明 materials 的内容。

2. *An effective agenda contains defined outcomes, logistics information for the meeting, attendee roles and responsibilities, a meeting time line and information needed for the meeting.* 一个有效的会议议程包括会议预期得到的结果，会议后勤保障，与会者职责，会议时间安排和其他会议相关信息。

   needed for the meeting 为过去分词短语作 information 的定语。

3. *It is important for meeting facilitators to hold a meeting in an appropriate setting that supports the work to be accomplished.* 会议组织者合理安排会议议程，对会议顺利举行很重要。

   It 是形式主语，真正的主语为不定式短语 to hold a meeting in an appropriate setting，setting 在本句中为名词，后接 that 引导的定语从句。

4. *State what information will be covered during the meeting and what information attendees should review prior to attending the meeting.* 阐明会议内容和与会者会前需要了解的信息。

   本句为祈使句。谓语动词 state 后接两个以 what 引导的宾语从句。what=the thing that…，兼有先行词和关系代词两项功能。

5. *The agenda should be distributed to participants several days in advance of a meeting, minimally 24 hours, so that participants have the opportunity to prepare for the meeting.* 会议议程要提前几天，至少提前24小时发给参会者，以便使他们有机会做好准备。

本句中 so that 引导的是目的状语从句。

Reading Comprehension

I. Discuss the following questions after reading the text.

1. Do you know the differences between meeting minutes and meeting agenda?

2. What is an agenda about?

3. When an agenda is necessary?

4. What information does an agenda contain?

5. Why is the restatement of meeting purpose important?

II. Choose the best answer to each of the following questions according to the text.

1. How does an agenda make a meeting productive?
    A. Agenda reduces the cost of a meeting.
    B. Agenda ensures the good use of time.
    C. Agenda is a combination of purposes.
    D. Agenda includes outcomes and logistics information.

2. Which is a correct statement of meeting purposes?
    A. Meeting purposes include instructing, persuading and making an agenda.
    B. Meeting purposes are desired outcomes.
    C. Meeting purposes can not support the outcomes.
    D. Meeting purposes pave the way for the success of a meeting.

3. What kind of information concerning facilitator and note taker should be described in an agenda?
    A. Responsibilities.   B. Salary.
    C.Title.   D. Experiences.

4. What is the structure of a time line?
    A. A chart.
    B. Combination of rows and columns.
    C. Columns.
    D. The same as poster.

5. When the agenda should be sent to the attendees?
   A. 7 days before a meeting.
   B. Several days before a meeting.
   C. 1 day before a meeting.
   D. 24 days before a meeting.

Vocabulary and Structures

I. Find the definition in Column B that matches the words in Column A.

Column A	Column B
1. agenda	A. result
2. accomplish	B. a piece of work
3. define	C. to describe something correctly and thoroughly
4. outcome	D. the end or final part of something
5. restatement	E. achieve
6. participant	F. someone who is taking part in an activity or event
7. conclusion	G. a list of the subjects to be discussed at a meeting
8. assignment	H. stating something again

II. Make the best choice to fill in the blanks with the given options in the box.

> A. hold a meeting in a proper setting that supports the work to be done
> B. Knowing what information attendees have to prepare in advance
> C. it focuses members' time and effort to achieve the meeting purpose
> D. every presenter knows his responsibility
> E. stating the purpose can ensure the success of a meeting

An agenda is important in terms of the success of a meeting because 1) _____ . When you are making an agenda, bear in mind that 2) _____ . It is necessary for meeting facilitators to 3) _____ . An agenda should make it clear that 4) _____ . A time line, structured as rows and columns, can keep a meeting moving smoothly. 5) _____ will also lead to a successful meeting.

Text B

Pre-reading Task: Answer the following questions before reading the text.

1. Do you know anything about web conference?

2. How can you make a web conference successful?

3. Can you make a good web conference agenda?

How to Organize a Web Conference Agenda
—A step-by-step guide for organizing your online conference

The first step to any successful meeting is knowing its purpose, and sharing it with your participants. Web **conferences** are no different—in fact, an agenda that is professional and well **put together** will ensure that your participants see your online meeting **in the same light** as a **face-to-face** one.[1] This is particularly important when introducing colleagues or superiors to the web conferencing **format**, as they could worry that the Internet is too **informal** a place to do business.

Also, a great agenda will make your colleagues see that you have put a lot of thought into your online conference. **What's more**, it will set the **tone** for your meeting. Your participants will see that it is an important meeting with a clear goal to be achieved—be that closing an important deal or starting a new project.[2]

By following the tips below, you will be able to make your agenda a perfect introduction to your online meeting.

Keep it clean. You have learned how to **upload** videos to the Internet or use Photoshop, which doesn't mean that you need to try to impress your colleagues with an **over-the-top** meeting agenda.[3] Good agendas keep a focus on the content, and do not **distract** your meeting participants with **fancy fonts** or colorful pictures. Learn to create professional word **processor documents**, and keep your agenda easy on the eyes by using a simple font such as Arial or Times New Roman, font size 10 to 12 and a clean background.

Let your participants know how they can connect to the meeting —Even if you have already sent details on how the attendees can connect either by VoIP or dial-in[4], it's good to include that information again on the agenda. If this is the first time you meet online, it's also a good idea to include details on how log-in works. This means that you should let attendees know if **registering** for the online meeting tool is necessary, and if they will need a **headset** or regular phone to connect. **As a result**, your meeting will not be delayed by any technical problems. Also let your IT team know that the meeting will

---

conference *n.* 讨论（会），会议
put together 拼，组成整体
in the same light 相同地
face-to-face *adj.* 当面的
format *n.* （某事物的）总体安排，计划
informal *adj.* 非正式的
what's more 而且，此外
tone *n.* 某事物的格调或特性

upload *v.* 上传

over-the-top *adj.* 夸大其词的，过分的
distract *v.* 使某人分心
fancy *adj.* 色彩鲜艳的，复杂的
font *n.* 字体
processor *n.* （计算机）中央处理器
document *n.* 文件

register *v.* 登记，注册
headset *n.* 头戴式受话器；双耳式耳机
as a result 结果

take place, and include their contact details so if there are any IT-related questions, your attendees know where to go for help.

Include discussion topics in **chronological** order—As with any meeting agenda, it is important to include discussion topics in the order they will be discussed. But the web conferencing format lets you go one step further; if your meeting has a **presentation**, you can include **links** to it so your participants can **familiarize** themselves with its contents prior to the meeting, or you can create a **workspace** in an online **collaboration** tool so the attendees can **pitch in** on further discussions that they think are necessary to the meeting.

Add **hyperlinks**—if any portion of the meeting needs prior knowledge from your participants on a certain area, include a hyperlink to a **relevant** website that can teach more about the subject you will be discussing. **Alternatively**, you can even send hyperlinks to internal documents from your company, for easy reference. If, for example, you would like your attendees to have read a certain report in the **system**, all you have to do if you want to link is press CTRL+K, then choose the path do the document. It will show on the agenda in link form. Keep in mind that this only works if all attendees are on the same internal system or Virtual Private Network (VPN).[5]

Include participant details—So that all attendees know who will be in the meeting, it is good to include details such as the name, position and e-mail address for each participant. Also let your participants know who will be speaking during the web conference. Many online meeting tools do not have **webcam capabilities**, so it could be difficult to know who a presenter is when they are speaking.

Make time for a Q&A[6]—this is perhaps even more important than in face-to-face meetings, as participants in those can raise their hand to interrupt the speaker and ask a question.[7] In an online meeting, this isn't always possible, so making enough time for a Q&A **session** is very important.

Creating a great online meeting agenda is not difficult once you learn to use the meeting's format **in your favor**. Once your agenda has all the necessary information, you will be on your way to a smooth web conference.[8]

(753 words)

---

chronological *adj.* 按时间的前后顺序排列的

presentation *n.* 陈述
link *n.* 链接
familiarize *v.* 使某人/自己熟悉某事物
workspace *n.* 工作空间
collaboration *n.* 合作
pitch in 使劲地干起来
hyperlink *n.* 超链接
relevant *adj.* 有关的，切题的
alternatively *adv.* 二者择一地

system *n.* 系统

webcam *n.* 网络摄像头
capability *n.* 能力

session *n.* （进行某活动连续的）一段时间

in someone /something's favor 对某人/某事有利

Notes

1. *Web conferences are no different—in fact, an agenda that is professional and well put together will ensure that your participants see your online meeting in the same light as a face-to-face one.* 网络会议也不例外。事实上，一份设计合理、专业的会议议程能够使参会者把网络会谈和直接会谈同等看待。

    此句是复合句，第一个 that 引导定语从句修饰 agenda，第二个 that 引导动词 ensure 的宾语从句。结尾的 a face-to-face one 中，不定代词 one 指代 meeting。

2. *Your participants will see that it is an important meeting with a clear goal to be achieved—be that closing an important deal or starting a new project.* 有明确目标要实现，参会者就会认为会议很重要——可能是达成某项重要交易或开始一个新项目。

    ... that it is an important meeting... 是动词 see 的宾语从句。从句中的主语 it 指代上文中的 your meeting。破折号后面的 be that closing an important deal or starting a new project 是对 a clear goal 的内容进行说明。

3. *You have learned how to upload videos to the Internet or use Photoshop, which doesn't mean that you need to try to impress your colleagues with an over-the-top meeting agenda.* 虽然你已经学会如何上传视频到互联网，如何使用图像处理软件 Photoshop，但这不意味着你要用夸张的会议议程博得同事的青睐。

    Photoshop，简称 PS，一个图像处理软件。

    本句中 which 引导非限制性定语从句，指代前面整句话的内容，这个非限制性定语从句中又有一个由 that 引导的宾语从句。

4. VoIP or dial-in：VoIP（Voice over Internet Protocol），网络电话；dial-in，拨号电话。

5. Virtual Private Network (VPN)：虚拟私人网络，以公共网络为基础的私人通信网络（为保证在一般网络上的信息安全传输而使用信息安全和频道协议）。

6. a Q&A，即下文中的 a Q&A session，Q=question，A=answer，a Q&A session 即提问与回答问题时间。

7. *This is perhaps even more important than in face-to-face meetings, as participants in those can raise their hand to interrupt the speaker and ask a question.* 这对于网络会议更重要，因为在面对面的会议中参会者可以举手打断发言者然后提问。

    as 引导原因状语从句，those 后面省略了 face-to-face meetings，完整的句子应是 as participants in those face-to-face meetings can raise their hand...。

8. *Once your agenda has all the necessary information, you will be on your way to a smooth web conference.* 一旦你的会议议程具备所有必要信息，网络会议将会顺利进行。

    once 意为"一旦，一……就……"，引导条件状语从句。

Reading Comprehension

Decide whether the following statements are true (T) or false (F) according to the text.

(　　) 1. Internet is too informal to do business.

(　　) 2. You should draw participants' attention to the meeting not to a colorful agenda.

( ) 3. It is unnecessary to include contact information on an agenda.

( ) 4. Some hyperlinks can make an online meeting fun.

( ) 5. A Q&A session is needed as for web conference.

Vocabulary

Fill in the blanks with the given words or expressions. Change the form where necessary.

1. The two groups met for _____ talks. (informal)

2. They talked in low _____ . (tone)

3. The film _____ me from these problems for a while. (distract)

4. The little girl _____ she heard a noise downstairs. (fancy)

5. He is not really _____ with her poetry. (familiarize)

6. We received all the _____ information. (relevant)

7. There are a number of _____ between the two theories. (link)

8. You have all the _____ of doing this job well. (capability)

Section C / Extending Your English

I. Approaching the reading skill: guessing unknown words（猜测生词词义）2

在阅读理解中，如何解决生词难题？上一单元已经介绍过运用比较和对比、单词结构和上下文逻辑关系等方法理解生词，本单元将介绍另外几种方法：下定义、重述和以同义词、近义词为线索猜测词义。

阅读中会遇到一些不熟悉的术语、专有名词或生僻词。作者为了使读者能够正确理解它们，就得做出较浅显的解释或说明。因而，借助作者的定义或释义推断词义是最直接的办法。例如：

1. The enemy soldiers surrendered, that is, threw their weapons and walked out with their hands above their heads.

短语 that is 后面就是对 surrendered 的释义：扔出武器，双手举过头顶走出来。由此可知，surrender 是"投降"之意。

2. The word ecology means the study of the relationship between living things and their surroundings.

动词 means 后给出 ecology 的含义，根据这个含义可推知 ecology 意为"生态学"。

用来表示定义或释义的提示语有：mean, refer to, be defined as, be described as, be known as, be called, be termed, that is, or, in other words 等。如果能够熟知这些提示语，就可以为推测词义奠定基础。

或者也可以利用标点符号，如括号、冒号、破折号等为一些生词直接提供定义或解释，例如：

In Russia if we give flowers as a present, we have to give an odd number of them (one, three, five, etc.) because even number of flowers (two, four, six, etc.) are for funerals.

通过括号里的例子可知 odd number 意思是"奇数"，even number 意思是"偶数"。

为使自己的意思表达得更清楚，作者还常用同义词或近义词来解释另一个比较难的词或关键词。另外，有些作者在表达同一概念时喜欢用两个或更多的同义词或近义词。这些同义词或近义词为读者推断生词词义提供了线索。根据已知的词语，就不难推断出生词的词义来。例如：

1. All the members are of the same opinions. They are unanimous.

用 the same opinion 理解 unanimous，意思为"一致同意的"。

2. The new tax law supersedes, or replaces, the law that was in effect last year.

此句中，作者考虑到 supersede 一词可能是生词，就用 or 引出该词的一个比较常用的同义词 replace 来进行重述，读者可根据 replace 一词的词义推断出 supersede 一词的大概意思为"取代，接替"。

同义词或近义词的标志词有 or, like, as...as, the same as 等。

再看下面这些例子：

1. The cloth was made of muslin. Muslin is a strong cotton.（下定义，muslin 意为"平纹细布，棉布"）

2. The teacher stood behind a lectern. A lectern is a tall stand used to hold a book for the speaker.（下定义，lectern 意为"讲台"）

3. New England has some of the most of fickle, or changeable, weather in the country.（重述，fickle 意为"多变的，无常的"）

4. Mike's handwriting is not legible; that is, it is difficult to read.（重述，legible 意为"清晰的，易读的"）

5. Tornadoes (violent and destructive whirl wind) normally occur on hot, humid (a little wet) day.（下定义，tornado 和 humid 两词的词义都在括弧里被清楚地表述出来。tornado 即一种非常剧烈的、破坏性很大的旋转的风。很明显，这是"旋风、飓风"；humid 即有点湿，意为"潮湿的"）

II. Applying the reading skill

Read the following passage and choose the best answer for each of the questions after your reading.

The Advantages of an Agenda

Agendas are useful for many meetings such as those in government **institutions**, **nonprofit** organizations and businesses. An agenda is a list of topics to be introduced and discussed during a meeting. Agendas generally include a reading of the last meeting's minutes or notes, relevant **announcements**, a review of the topics for discussion and a roll call.[1] Although agendas take time to set up, in the long run they can save time and resources.

Agendas provide an **outline** of discussion topics. The outline prevents the **moderator** or members of the meeting from forgetting important topics to introduce. When all topics are thoroughly discussed, valuable decisions can be made as a group during the

institution n. 机构
nonprofit adj. 非营利的

announcement n. 公告

outline n. 要点；大纲
moderator n. 会议主席，仲裁者

meeting instead of hurriedly making plans outside the meeting.[2] **Input** and suggestions from a variety of **perspectives** improves the quality of performance by members.

Agendas provide an opportunity to inform members through announcements about critical events, goals and tasks. Agendas enable members who might not have **access** to everyone in the organization to announce important news and hear news of interest. Without an agenda, announcements may not be communicated to all the members, which can cause confusion or misunderstanding. Agendas also **recap previous** meetings to help members review the progress made and narrow the focus for the current meeting.

Agendas generally mention items to be discussed for the next meeting. This gives the members a chance to prepare the discussion topics before the meeting. At many meetings, **outspoken** members **are** more than **eager to** participate while reserved individuals may be more **hesitant**. However, knowing what is going to be discussed enables members to research topics of interests, think about how the topics apply to their **realm** and then make **thoughtful**, quality contributions at the meeting.[3]

An agenda prioritizes the most important activities, increases productivity and focuses the members. The only presence of an agenda creates a formal **atmosphere** and **discourages** members from wasting time. An agenda also sets the objectives and gives the members a goal. This organizes the thoughts of the members, direction of the meeting and the action after the meeting.

A **collection** of past agendas is an **ideal** record for **external** and internal institutions, organizations and the public for viewing the progress of your organization. The **documentation** helps the public and organization members assess past decisions, remind them of previous events or important figures and **formulate** feasible goals. With these advantages, agenda is definitely worth the time and effort.

(413 words)

---

input n. 意见
perspective n. 看法

access n. （使用某物或接近某人的）机会

recap v. 简要地复述
previous adj. （时间或顺序上）在先的；先前的

outspoken adj. 直言的；坦率的
(be) eager to 热切的
hesitant adj. 犹豫的
realm n. （活动或兴趣的）领域
thoughtful adj. 深思熟虑的

atmosphere n. 气氛
discourage v. 设法阻止（某事物）

collection n. 成堆物品
ideal adj. 理想的，最合适的
external adj. 外面的
documentation n. 文件
formulate v. 制定

Notes

1. *Agendas generally include a reading of the last meeting's minutes or notes, relevant announcements, a review of the topics for discussion and a roll call.* 会议议程包含前次会议纪要，此次会议相关通知，讨论话题介绍和点名。

    此句中介词短语 for discussion 做 topics 的定语。roll call 意为"点名"。

2. *When all topics are thoroughly discussed, valuable decisions can be made as a group during the*

meeting instead of hurriedly making plans outside the meeting. 所有话题充分讨论后，会议全体成员在会议期间便可做出有价值的决策，不必会后匆忙决议。

此句中 when 引导的状语从句和主句都使用了被动语态，以使动作承受者得到强调。instead of 意为"而不是……与之相反，代替"。短语介词 instead of 隐含了对其后面所接成分的否定。

3. *However, knowing what is going to be discussed enables members to research topics of interests, think about how the topics apply to their realm and then make thoughtful, quality contributions at the meeting.* 但是，事先了解会议内容有助于会议成员对感兴趣的内容提前研究，结合自己领域加以思考，开会时提供全面，优质的信息。

knowing what is going to be discussed 是句子的主语，谓语动词是 enable。thoughtful 和 quality 都是 contribution 的定语。

Exercise: Read the text again and choose the closest expression of each underlined word by using the reading skill.

1. An <u>agenda</u> is a list of topics to be introduced and discussed during a meeting.
    A. schedule   B. notice   C. document   D. poster

2. The outline prevents the <u>moderator</u> or members of the meeting from forgetting important topics to introduce.
    A. photographer   B. stuff   C. speaker   D. supervisor

3. When all topics are <u>thoroughly</u> discussed, that is, participants have a full discussion of topics, ...
    A. excitedly   B. loudly   C. completely   D. eagerly

4. Without an agenda, announcements may not be communicated to all the members, which can cause <u>confusion</u> or misunderstanding.
    A. fight   B. anger   C. disorder   D. understanding

5. Agendas also <u>recap</u> previous meetings to help members review the progress made and narrow the focus for the current meeting.
    A. return   B. repeat   C. recall   D. introduce

Section D Self-evaluation

After learning this unit, I have grasped

Items	100%	80%	60%	Below 50%
Words				
Grammar				
Reading				

Notes to this unit:

Unit 7

Meetings

Learning Objectives

In this unit, you will learn

- to understand the importance of conducting successful meetings;
- to get basic information about meetings;
- to master the new words and expressions;
- to apply the reading skill—scanning to locate specifically required information.

Section A / Lead-in

I. Can you name these types of business meetings?

Directions: Match the words or expressions in the box with the types of the business meetings.

(1)

(2)

(3)

(4)

(5)

(6)

```
A. teleconference        B. face to face meeting    C. videoconference
D. criticism meeting     E. group meeting           F. one on one meeting
```

II. Describe the above pictures.

Directions: Work in pairs to describe the above meetings you know best.

Section B / Embracing English

Text A

Pre-reading Task: Answer the following questions before reading the text.

1. What are the main functions of business meetings?

2. How is an effective meeting running?

3. What is the objective of status meeting

About Business Meetings

Business meetings can either be a useful way to communicate information with important **staff** members or a channel to share valuable company resources.[1] Organizing and conducting effective meetings is a requirement for many job descriptions. There are several types of meetings. Team and status meetings[2] are two of the most common.

Business meetings occur for different purposes. Depending on the purpose and the type of meetings, there are **specific** formats and objectives for each. Team meetings are one of the most regularly scheduled meetings in the business environment. Conducting team meetings is a test of leadership abilities. Many managers simply call a meeting, expect everyone to be prepared for anything to be discussed, and send out no agenda for what to expect. Scheduling meetings with little thought for planning or a clear objective **is sure to** fail.[3]

So how is an effective meeting run? For starters, careful planning, a stated objective and a detailed agenda should be sent to all participants at least a week before the meeting. The objective should be short and clear. Keep the meeting within a reasonable time period. Unless the meeting is planned to decide a process or solve a problem, the length should not **exceed** one hour. Provide time limits for each agenda item.

The meeting should also start on time. Each agenda item should be discussed, being careful to keep the discussion **related to** the listed topic. If the discussion is not finishing anything in the way of providing essential information or solving a problem—move on to the next topic.[4] If a new topic leads to further discussion, **take note of** the topic and include the item on the agenda for the next meeting.

Status meetings are handled differently. Project Managers often use status meeting to **revise** project plans, update **stakeholders**, and assess the importance among different tasks. The agenda for these types of meetings is usually much more specific than a general meeting. Status is reported on a project, account, or client. The objective for this type of meeting is for all participants to report progress on their own tasks in order to assess the status of the entire project.

So how can project managers conduct successful meetings? Having a strategy will be a must to improve communication and information sharing and create less anxiety among meeting participants.[5] It will also create more focused teams and less wasted time. Project Managers will develop more effective communication and leadership skills, and will find that their project plans will be more clear and up-to-date.

In the high-tech age, technology has provided effective tools to conduct meeting and make the best use of meeting time. Microsoft Project and Microsoft Outlook provide valuable tools to schedule, share information, and update project tasks—sometimes free you from the need to even have a face-to-face meeting. Microsoft Word includes an agenda tool which can help create an agenda with all the necessary information. Using these tools with the tips contained above will ensure a successful meeting. It will also develop effective leadership and communication skills as well.

Scheduling a meeting is simple—but does not ensure that it will serve a useful purpose. It is a misunderstanding that technology produces wonderful meetings. Too many meeting organizers schedule meetings with little thought to planning and organizing, which finally fails to achieve the aims of meetings.

Business Meetings serve a **vital** role in **disseminating** information, providing project status, and **facilitating** communications between team members. Conducting them in the most effective manner fulfills the goals set out by the organizer, and ensures that company time and resources are not wasted.

(619 words)

New Words and Expressions

staff /stɑːf/	n.	the group of people who work for an organization（全体）职员；（全体）工作人员
status /ˈsteɪtəs/	n.	state or condition with respect to circumstances; a situation at a particular time 情形；状况；形势
specific /spəˈsɪfɪk/	adj.	relating to one thing and not others; particular 特殊的，特定的
exceed /ɪkˈsiːd/	v.	to be greater than a number or amount, or to go past an allowed limit 超过；超出
revise /rɪˈvaɪz/	v.	to look at or consider again an idea, piece of writing, etc. in order to correct or improve it 修改，修正
stakeholder /ˈsteɪkˌhəʊldər/	n.	a person such as an employee, customer, or citizen who is involved with an organization, society, etc. and therefore has responsibilities towards it and an interest in its success 参与者；相关人员；利益共享者
vital /ˈvaɪtəl/	adj.	extremely important 极其重要的，必不可少的
disseminate /dɪˈsemɪneɪt/	v.	to spread or give out something, especially news, information, ideas, etc., to a lot of people 散播；宣传
facilitate /fəˈsɪlɪteɪt/	v.	to make something possible or easier 促进；帮助
(be) sure to do		必定（做）
related to		与……有关
take note of		注意

Notes

1. **Business meetings can either be a useful way to communicate information with important staff members or a channel to share valuable company resources.** 商务会议可以成为与重要职员交流信息的有效手段或分享公司宝贵资源的渠道。

    此句中的 either... or... 为并列结构，either be a useful way to... 和 or (be) a channel to... 形成并列关系，且两个短语中都带有不定式结构作后置定语。

2. *status meeting* 情况通报会；通气会，指由团队负责人召集，通报工作任务进展状况的会议，内容常为报告团队任务的完成进展状况，如在某特定时间完成任务的 50%、70% 等。

3. *Scheduling meetings with little thought for planning or a clear objective is sure to fail.* 没有考虑计划和明确目标的会议安排是注定要失败的。

  此句的主语结构是 is sure to fail 之前的部分，该结构是由中心词语 Scheduling meetings 加 with 引导的介宾结构作后置定语，且这一介宾结构中又包含 for 引导的介宾结构：for planning or (for) a clear objective。

4. *If the discussion is not finishing anything in the way of providing essential information or solving a problem—move on to the next topic.* 如果讨论不能达到提供必要的信息，或解决问题的目的，那就继续下一个话题。

  in the way of 后接 or 连接并列的 v-ing 结构，其完整形式可以理解为 in the way of providing essential information or (in the way) of solving a problem。

5. *Having a strategy will be a must to improve communication and information sharing and create less anxiety among meeting participants.* 为了改善沟通、促进信息交流和减少与会人员的焦虑情绪，策略是必不可少的。

  此句中 must 是名词，作表语，意思是"必须做的事，必不可少的事物"；其后的不定式短语是后置定语，此不定式结构中 improve communication and information and information sharing 与 create less anxiety among meeting participants 是并列关系。

Reading Comprehension

I. Answer the following questions according to the text.

1. What are the most common types of meetings?

2. What is the objective for status meeting?

3. How can project managers conduct successful meetings?

4. What purposes do business meetings occur for?

5. What effective tools can be provided to conduct meeting?

II. Choose the best answer for each of the following questions according to the text.

1. What is a requirement for many job descriptions?
 A. Organizing and conducting effective meetings.
 B. Educational background.
 C. Working experience.
 D. Personal hobbies.

2. The objective of meetings should be _____ .

   A. long and detail

   B. short and clear

   C. clear and coherent

   D. concise and detail

3. How long is the reasonable time period of the business meetings?

   A. Half hour.

   B. One hour.

   C. One and a half hours.

   D. Two hours.

4. What to do if the discussion is not finishing anything in the way of providing essential information or solving a problem during the meeting?

   A. Go on the discussion.

   B. Stop the discussion.

   C. Move on to the next topic.

   D. Change the topic of the discussion.

5. What makes the meeting organizers fail to achieve the aims of meetings?

   A. With more thought to planning and organizing when they schedule meetings.

   B. With more thought to designing when they schedule meetings.

   C. With little thought to designing when they schedule meetings.

   D. With little thought to planning and organizing when they schedule meetings.

Vocabulary and Structures

I. Find the definition in Column B that matches the words in Column A.

Column A	Column B
1. staff	A. to spread information or ideas to as many people as possible
2. status	B. the people who work for an organization
3. specific	C. a state or condition of something at a particular time
4. agenda	D. a specific thing, person, or group is one particular thing, person, or group
5. participant	E. a list of matters to be discussed at a meeting
6. revise	F. someone who is taking part in an activity or event
7. vital	G. to look at or consider again an idea, piece of writing, etc in order to correct or improve it
8. disseminate	H. extremely important and necessary for something to succeed or exist

Unit 7 Meetings

II. Make the best choice to fill in the blanks with the given options in the box.

> A. Team and status meetings are two of the most common
> B. assess the importance among different tasks
> C. company time and resources are not wasted
> D. a channel to share valuable company resources
> E. facilitating communications between team members

Business meetings can either be a useful way to communicate information with important staff members or 1)_____ . There are several types of meetings. 2)_____ . Team meetings are one of the most regularly scheduled meetings in the business environment. Project Managers often use status meeting to revise project plans, update stakeholders, and 3)_____ . Business Meetings serve a vital role in disseminating information, providing project status, and 4)_____ . Conducting business meetings in the most effective manner can fulfills the goals set out by the organizer, and ensures that 5)_____ .

Text B

Pre-reading Task: Answer the following questions before reading the text.

1. Do you think people really enjoy attending meetings? Why or why not?

2. How to increase attendance for business meetings?

3. Which factors should be considered when selecting the location of business meetings?

Increase Attendance for Business Meetings

The most important step to overcoming fears about a lack of **attendance** at a meeting or to increase the RSVP(please reply) list is to realize that people really do enjoy attending **seminars** and meetings.[1] By attending business meetings, the participant gets a chance to learn new information and communicate with **peers** and leaders in their field. The most successful meetings create a warm, friendly environment for everyone—and that is why they enjoy attending. So the knowledge of ways to increase attendance for meetings is essential for organizers.

A great agenda is the first on the list. Once **hosts** understand

> attendance n. 到场；出席
> seminar n. 专题讨论会
>
> peer n. 同龄人；社会地位相同的人
>
> host n. 主持人

that people enjoy attending meetings, it is important to create a program that is worth attending.² The agenda should be focused on a single topic and not confuse attendees. For example, the following sample half day seminar schedule considers the meeting attendees' needs:

8:00 a.m. Arrivals and Breakfast
8:45 a.m. Welcome Message
9:00 a.m. **Keynote Speaker**
10:00 a.m. Break
10:15 a.m. Discussion
11:30 a.m. Closing Speech

Despite the best agenda, meeting attendees have likes as to when they want to attend such programs and when they cannot. Consider the following when scheduling dates and times for your event: attendees prefer morning schedules for seminars; attendees prefer **appreciation** events immediately after work; Tuesdays and Thursdays are popular meeting days; avoid holding meetings on Fridays if possible; avoid scheduling meetings on holidays and the eve of holidays.

A wonderful and convenient location will help attract participants. Most business meetings are held in hotels and that is not so unique. But not all hotels are the same, and hotels are not the only **available** places. The main point here is to select a location where your guests want to go.³ After all, if they are long for the place you choose, they will attend the meeting and enjoy it. Consider the following **factors**:

Select a venue that is near the majority of attendees.
Select a venue where attendees would enjoy themselves.
Select a venue that is experienced at hosting similar events.

Successful meetings have a specific topic and **target** audience for that message. It is valuable to make a guest list that includes appropriate attendees, even if they are ranked in order of importance. Too often, hosts will compile a master list of potential guests and open the meeting to the masses. This will work if you are trying to fill seats based on the numbers game.

However, the business meeting shouldn't be viewed as a direct mail effort with 1-3% RSVP rates.

A final thought about attendees: try to invite person of similar rank and experience to the meeting.

One of the keys to achieving attendance to meeting is by

---

keynote speaker *n.* 主讲人，主题发言人

appreciation *n.* 欣赏，鉴赏；赏识

available (for/to) *adj.* 可用的，在手边的；可利用的

factor *n.* 因素；要素

target *n.* 目标

inviting people early, and continue reminding them about the event even if they have **confirmed** attendance. It's important to create excitement around the event. **Traditional** printed invitations are appropriate, and it is now generally acceptable to rely on technology to send your invitation. Try this method:

Mention the event to guests before sending invites.

Send a save the date early in the planning process (paper or electronic).

Send a detailed invitation, including agenda **highlights** (paper or electronic).

Forward the detailed invitation again with a personalized note (electronic).

Formally call guests and extend a personal invite to the event.

A physical invitation—whether printed or electronic—is nice, but it shouldn' be viewed as a replacement for a personally extended invitation (unless you are planning a large **symposium** or with 500 or more attendees). This is the step that makes most hosts crazy … they do not want to dial for attendees.

It is helpful to share this responsibility. The guest list of an event is often created from contact lists that are **maintained** by a variety of individuals, and those individuals with the closest relationships to the invitees should extend a direct invitation to their own guests.

Everyone has attended good meetings and bad meetings, and the same holds true for seminars and other appreciation events. Lucky for planners, people more often enjoy the meetings they attend. The key here is to help your client establish a reputation for delivering excellent business programs. Simple as it may seem, if someone enjoyed attending your last series of meetings, he or she is more likely to attend future programs.

Because people attend meetings to gather new information, many attendees appreciate receiving additional **handouts** and materials that may have been referenced by presenters and other folks within your organization. It is an excellent opportunity to share that information with follow thank you messages to those who attended the event. The thank you note and follow up communications is something that many organizations often **overlook**, but noticed by guests. (782 words)

---

confirm *v.* 证实；确定
traditional *adj.* 传统的；惯例的

highlight *n.* 最突出（或最精彩）的部分；最重要（或最有趣）的事情（+of）

symposium *n.* 讨论会；座谈会

maintain *v.* 维持；保持

handout *n.* 讲课提纲；讲义

overlook *v.* 看漏；忽略

Notes

1. *The most important step to overcoming fears about a lack of attendance at a meeting or to increase the RSVP (please reply) list is to realize that people really do enjoy attending seminars and meetings.* 要解决对参会人数不足的担忧或提升对邀请函的回复率，最重要的一步是要相信人们是乐于参加研讨和会议的。

    RSVP 是法语 Répondez s'il vous plait. 的缩写，意思是"请答复"。接到邀请（无论是请柬或邀请信）后，能否出席要尽早答复对方，以便主人安排。一般来说，对注有 R.S.V.P.（请答复）字样的，无论出席与否，均应迅速答复。

2. *Once hosts understand that people enjoy attending meetings, it is important to create a program that is worth attending.* 一旦主办方明白人们是喜欢参加会议的，制定一个值得参加的会议日程安排就很重要了。

    本句的主句是 it is important to create a program that is worth attending。it 为形式主语，不定式短语 to create a program... 为真正的主语，在这个不定式短语中又包含了一个 that 引导的定语从句，修饰、限定动词不定式的宾语 program，而句首的 once 为连词引导一个条件状语从句。

3. *The main point here is to select a location where your guests want to go.* 重点是选择一个客人想去的地点。

    to select a location..., 不定式短语作表语；名词 location 后接关系副词 where 引导的定语从句，说明地点。

Reading Comprehension

Decide whether the following statements are true (T) or false (F) according to the text.

(   ) 1. The most successful meetings create a warm, friendly environment for everyone.

(   ) 2. The agenda should be focused on a single topic and not confuse attendees.

(   ) 3. Try to invite person of different rank and experience to the meeting.

(   ) 4. Generally, people do not enjoy the meetings they attend.

(   ) 5. The thank you note and follow up communications is something that many organizations often notice, but overlooked by guests.

Vocabulary

Fill in the blanks with the given words or expressions. Change the form where necessary.

1. Over 2000 people were in _____ at yesterday's demonstration. (attendance)

2. Publishers and writers from 13 countries attended a series of _____ . (seminar)

3. It helps children to develop an _____ of poetry and literature. (appreciation)

4. Funds are _____ to assist teachers who want to attend the conference. (available)

5. New evidence has _____ the first witness's story. (confirm)

6. It is _____ not to eat meat on Good Friday. (tradition)

7. The hotel prides itself on _____ high standards. (maintain)

8. Nobody could _____ the fact that box office sales were down. (overlook)

Section C Extending Your English

I. Approaching the reading skill: scanning to locate specifically required information（查读）1

　　查读（scanning）是一种快速阅读技巧，目的在于从阅读材料中查找出所需要的某项或某些特定的信息。运用查读的方法捕捉具体信息，可以提高阅读效率。

　　查读是要从大量的资料中查找某一具体事实或某一项特定信息——如人物、事件、时间、地点、数字等——而对于其他无关部分则可以略去不读。运用这种方法，我们就能在最短时间内掠过尽可能多的阅读材料，定位到所需要的信息。例如，在机场寻找某次班机的飞行时刻，在图书馆查找书刊的目录，在文献中查找某一日期、名字、数字或号码等，都可以运用这种方法。

　　作为一种快速寻找信息的阅读技巧，查读带有明确的目的性，是有针对性地选择问题的答案。因此，可以把整段的文字直接映入大脑，不必逐句地过目。视线在阅读材料上掠过时，一旦发现有关的内容，将它记住或摘录下。

　　可以利用下列技巧，更有效地进行查读。

　　1. 利用章节标题和说明

　　查读之前，首先看看文章标题或章节标题，确定是否包含自己所需要的信息，或者哪一部分包含信息，这样可以直接进入那个部分查找。

　　2. 利用资料的编排形式

　　词典、索引、电话号码簿等是按字母顺序排列的，电视节目是按日期和时间排列的，历史资料是按年代排列的。在查读时，一定要明确资料的排列方式，以提高效率，避免盲目查询。

　　3. 抓关键词

　　找到包含所需信息的部分时，要注意与查读的具体信息有关系的关键词。

Practice: Scanning for information

　　　　Look over the bus schedule quickly, and then answer the questions.

Hudson Bus company
YORKTOWN—BOXFORD

DEPARTING	TIME OF DEPARTURE	ARRIVING	TIME OF ARRIVAL
YORKTOWN	6:00 a.m.	BOXFORD	8:00 a.m.
BOXFORD	8:30 a.m.	YORKTOWN	10:30 a.m.

Reading Skills 1

DEPARTING	TIME OF DEPARTURE	ARRIVING	TIME OF ARRIVAL
YORKTOWN	11:00 a.m.	BOXFORD	1:00 p.m.
BOXFORD	1:30 p.m.	YORKTOWN	3:30 p.m.
YORKTOWN	4:00 p.m.	BOXFORD	6:00 p.m.

Circle the correct answer to complete each sentence

1) The first bus from Yorktown: Departing time is _____ .

   A. 11:00 a.m.   B. 4:00 p.m.   C. 6:00 a.m.

2) There are _____ morning bus trips to Boxford.

   A. one   B. two   C. three

3) The last bus to Yorktown: Departing time is _____ .

   A. 6:00 a.m.   B. 4:00 p.m.   C. 1:30 p.m.

II. Applying the reading skill

Read the following passage and answer the questions according to the text.

Make Business Meetings Fun

Very few people look forward to attending a business meeting. Depending on the subject and the participants, business meetings can be boring, and bored participants are usually not active participants. There are some strategies that meeting planners and managers can use to liven up business meetings, or even to make them fun. When your meetings are fun, your employees and colleagues are more likely to look forward to attending them and to **participate** to the best of their abilities.

Start off the meeting with a fun ice-breaking game, preferably one that doesn't have anything to do with the agenda of the meeting. The best games **arouse** the interests of the meeting participants and **inject** humor into the meeting room. Everyone loves a free meal, and offering a meal or **snack** during the meeting can relax everyone and create a good feeling. Try a **make-your-own**[1] ice cream **sundae** bar, or order some pizza.

Give everyone a small toy to play with. Even adults like toys, and throwing a rubber ball during a brainstorming period can help keep the ideas flowing and help everyone get a turn to speak. Modeling clay, toy cars, building blocks and other

---

participate v. 参加；参与

arouse v. 唤起；激动；使奋发
inject v. 引入；投入
snack n. 小吃，点心
make-your-own adj. 自制的
sundae n. 圣代冰淇淋

inexpensive toys can help meeting participants loosen up and have fun.

Celebrate the conclusion of a successful project, a new client or even an employee's personal progress. Serve sparkling water or cider in glasses, or simply offer a round of **applause**; the idea is to build and express a goodwill.

Take the meeting outside. Moving outside the regular meeting room can help get ideas flowing and help the participants think creatively.

Ask your employees what they think would make the meetings more fun[2]. You might get answers like "Fewer meetings" or "Shorter meetings," but you also might get some good ideas about what your employees actually want.

A break is of help. Sometimes just stopping the business **portion** of the meeting and taking a quick break can refresh participants.

Keep in mind that not all employees will be interested in the idea of fun meetings. Some people just want to attend the meeting, deal with the business at hand and get back to work. Don't force people to laugh and have fun, but let it happen naturally.

The best way to keep your employees eager to attend meetings is to make them useful and worthwhile. Always have a purpose for your meeting, and stay within the **allotted** meeting time. Don't waste time on items unrelated to the meeting agenda. Making your meetings fun won't matter if the attendees feel like you are wasting their timing less boring. (432 words)

celebrate *v.* 庆祝

applause *n.* 鼓掌欢迎；喝彩

portion (of) *n.* （一）部分

allot (to) *v.* 分配；分配给

Notes

1. make-your-own，这是一个由不带不定式符号 to 的短语临时组合构成的形容词。在现代英语中，以这样灵活的方式构成的形容词因为其简单明了而越来越受欢迎。
2. *Ask your employees what they think would make the meetings more fun*，询问员工的想法会使会议更轻松有趣。
   本句为祈使句充当主语从句，而在主语从句中又嵌套了一个 what 引导的宾语从句。

Exercise: Answer the following questions according to the text.

1. How many strategies of living up business meetings were mentioned in the passages?

2. What is the best way to keep your employees eager to attend meeting?

Section D / Self-evaluation

After learning this unit, I have grasped

Items	100%	80%	60%	Below 50%
Words				
Grammar				
Reading				

Notes to this unit:

Unit 8

Business Travel

Learning Objectives

In this unit, you will learn

- to understand the importance of making travel arrangements;
- to get basic information about business travel;
- to master the new words and expressions related to travel arrangements;
- to apply the reading skill—scanning to locate specifically required information.

Section A / Lead-in

I. Can you name these types of business travel?

Directions: Match the words or expressions in the box with the types of business travel.

(1)　　　　　　　　　(2)　　　　　　　　　(3)

(4)　　　　　　　　　(5)　　　　　　　　　(6)

> A. self-driving traveling　　　　B. travel by plane　　　　C. check-in
> D. visit some places of interest　E. enjoy life with local people　F. eat in a restaurant

II. Describe the above pictures.

Directions: Work in pairs to describe the above pictures. (What are these people doing? Where are they?)

Section B / Embracing English

Text A

Pre-reading Task: Answer the following questions before reading the text.

1. How important are travel arrangements & itinerary?

2. How to make travel arrangement & itinerary?

3. Why should we share a copy of the itinerary with close family members or friends?

How to Make Travel Arrangements & Itinerary

Travel arrangements and an **itinerary** are two basic **requirements** for any trip. Although many people **rely on** travel agencies to organize these things for them, with the **availability** of cheaper self-serve travel options online, this has become a task that modern travelers must master.[1] Making your own travel arrangements allows you **flexibility** and sometimes cheaper prices if you research your options carefully. **In addition**, designing an itinerary allows you to maximize your time spent at your destination and make sure it fits into your schedule.

So how to make travel arrangements & itinerary? Chose your destination. If you don't know where you are going, then the other steps will make no sense. If you are planning a vacation and are unsure of where to go, you should initially consider your **budget** for the trip and the time you have available. Finally, **take into account** your **preferences**: beach or mountains, countryside or **cosmopolitan** city, child-friendly or adults-only.

Decide on the method of **transportation**. How are you going to get to where you want to go: car, train, plane, boat? Which class or comfort level? There's usually first, business and coach for planes, or first and second class for trains, for example. The transportation you choose will affect the next step because it will involve getting from your arrival point to your lodging.

Reserve lodging. This might be a hotel—ranging from one to five stars—a guest house, a bed and breakfast or even a hostel. Ensure you have lodging for each night of your trip before you leave. You don't want to run into any unpleasant surprises if you count on finding something along the way. Look for lodging that accommodates budget and needs, and make sure that it is located in a strategic point for your trip. For example, if it's a business trip, you may prefer the lodging to be close to the office where you are working. Or you may prefer to be close to the airport so that you may easily access your lodging once you land and quickly check out before **departure**.[2] In addition, you should make sure your lodging is easily **accessible** from your arrival point.

Decide on meals and sightseeing. When planning a trip, your budget for meals plays an important role. If part of your trip is to **indulge** in local **gastronomy**, this step should be carefully planned. Research the restaurants you are interested in and call ahead to make **reservations**, if necessary. In addition, you should **calculate** any tourist visits and sightseeing into the travel arrangements, if necessary. For example, if you are headed to Paris, you might want to reserve a visit to the Eiffel Tower ahead of time, so as to avoid standing in line to buy tickets.

Making an itinerary is much like making a calendar for your trip. Once travel arrangements have been made, you can start by writing "Day 1" on a sheet of paper next to your date of departure. Continue doing so for every day of the trip. The last day you mark will be the day of arrival back home.

Choose how specific you want to be. You may be able to calculate every aspect of the trip down to the minute if you are on a one-day business trip, or be rather **loose** if you are on a weeklong vacation.[3] Start filling out the calendar with what you do know: date and time of departure, date and time of arrival, **approximate** travel time between place of arrival and lodging, planned activities and so on.

Leave room for **error**. Things happen when we travel, including bad weather, traffic jams and overbooked hotels. Leaving some room for error, or at least having a backup plan, can save you a headache later on. If you are going on vacation, it is good to make a "rainy day" or **alternate** plan if many of the main activities you have planned are outdoors.

Share a copy of the itinerary with close family members or friends. Particularly if you are going abroad, this may be a good idea in case in the case of an **emergency**.

New Words and Expressions

itinerary /aɪ'tɪnərəri/	n.	a detailed plan or route of a journey 旅程；路线；行程安排
requirement /rɪ'kwaɪəmənt/	n.	something that you must do, or something you need 需要；必需品，要求；必要条件；规定（+for）
availability /əˌveɪlə'bɪlɪti/	n.	the fact that something can be bought, used, or reached, or how much it can be 可得到的东西（或人）
flexible /'fleksɪbl/	adj.	able to change or be changed easily according to the situation 可弯曲的，易弯曲的；柔韧的；有弹性的
budget /'bʌdʒɪt/	n.	the amount of money you have available to spend 预算；预算费；生活费，经费（+for）
preference /'prefərəns/	n.	the fact that you like something or someone more than another thing or person 偏爱；偏爱的人或事物
cosmopolitan /ˌkɒzmə'pɒlɪtən/	adj.	containing or having experience of people and things from many different parts of the world 世界性的，国际性的
transportation /ˌtrænspɔː'teɪʃən/	n.	a vehicle or system of vehicles, such as buses, trains, etc. for getting from one place to another 运输工具；交通车辆
departure /dɪ'pɑːtʃə/	n.	the fact of a person or vehicle, etc. leaving somewhere 离开；出发，起程（+for）
accessible /ək'sesəbl/	adj.	able to be reached or easily got 可（或易）接近的；可（或易）进入的
indulge /ɪn'dʌldʒ/	v.	to allow yourself or another person to have something enjoyable, especially more than is good for you 使自己高兴一下；让自己享受一下（+in）
gastronomy /gæs'trɒnmi/	n.	the art and knowledge involved in preparing and eating good food 美食法
reservation /ˌrezə'veɪʃən/	n.	an arrangement in which something such as a seat on an aircraft or a table at a restaurant is kept for you 预订
calculate /'kælkjʊleɪt/	v.	to form an opinion about something by using all the information 计划，打算；把……考虑进去
loose /luːs/	adj.	describes things that are not fixed or held together or to anything else 不严密的，不确切的，不明确的

approximate /ə'prɒksɪmət/	*adj.*	not completely accurate but close 大约的，大概的	
error /'erər/	*n.*	a mistake 错误，差错	
alternate /'ɒltəneɪt/	*adj.*	an alternative plan or method is one that you can use if you do not want to use another one 供选择的；供替换的	
emergency /ɪ'mɜːdʒənsi/	*n.*	something dangerous or serious, such as an accident, which happens suddenly or unexpectedly and needs fast action in order to avoid harmful result 紧急情况；突发事件；非常时刻	
rely on		依赖，依靠	
take into account		考虑到；体谅	

Notes

1. *Although many people rely on travel agencies to organize these things for them, with the availability of cheaper self-serve travel options online, this has become a task that modern travelers must master.* 尽管很多人还是依靠旅行社来为他们安排旅行日程，但由于便宜的在线自助旅游选择很多，安排旅行日程已经成了现代旅行者必须掌握的一门功课。

    这个句子的主句是 this has become a task that modern travelers must master。Although 从句中的 these things 指的是本文第一个句子中的 travel arrangements and an itinerary；介词短语 with the availability of cheaper self-serve travel options online 用来表示原因；而主句中的主语 this 则指代下文中的 Making your own travel arrangements。

2. *Or you may prefer to be close to the airport so that you may easily access your lodging once you land and quickly check out before departure.* 或者你更愿意住得离机场近一些，以便你一降落，就会很容易地找到住所，而离开时也能快速退房。

    or 是表示选择性的并列连词，在此用以引出另一种可能性。句中还包含一个以 so that 引导的目的状语从句。

3. *You may be able to calculate every aspect of the trip down to the minute if you are on a one-day business trip, or be rather loose if you are on a weeklong vacation.* 如果你要安排一次为时一天的商务旅程，你可能会将行程的方方面面精确计算到每一分钟；但是如果你有一周的假期，那么行程就相对宽松了。

    并列连词 or 在此连接两个句子。前后两个分句有共同的主语 you，且共用情态动词 may，所以在 or 后面的分句中省略了主语和情态动词。

Reading Comprehension

I. Answer the following questions according to the text.

1. What are the basic requirements for any trip?

2. What are the main functions of making your own travel arrangement?

3. How to make travel arrangements & itinerary?

4. Which type of lodging you prefer when you are on a business trip?

5. Why should you leave room for error in designing an itinerary?

II. Choose the best answer to each of the following questions according to the text.

1. What has become a task that modern travelers must master?
   A. Travel arrangements.
   B. Travel itinerary.
   C. Travel agencies.
   D. Travel arrangements itinerary.

2. Which one is right in the following sentences?
   A. If you know where you are going, then the other steps will make no sense.
   B. Deciding on the method of transportation is not important to make travel arrangement and itinerary.
   C. According to the text, it is not necessary to have lodging for each night of your trip before you leave.
   D. When planning a trip, your budget for meals plays an important role.

3. If part of your trip is to indulge in local gastronomy, _____ should be carefully planned.
   A. your budget for meals   B. deciding on sightseeing
   C. reserving restaurants   D. buying the tickets

4. Making an itinerary is much like making a _____ for your trip.
   A. calendar   B. requirement
   C. schedule   D. agenda

5. Why should you leave room for error?
   A. For emergency.   B. For traffic jams.
   C. It can save you a headache later on.   D. It is good to make an alternate plan.

Vocabulary and Structures

I. Find the definition in Column B that matches the words in Column A.

Column A	Column B
1. arrangement	A. a vehicle or system of vehicles, such as buses, trains, etc. for getting from one place to another
2. transportation	B. able to be reached or easily got
3. maximize	C. If you reserve something such as a seat on an aircraft or a table at a restaurant, you arrange for it to be kept for your use

4. budget	D. something dangerous or serious, such as an accident, which happens suddenly or unexpectedly and needs fast action in order to avoid harmful results
5. reserve	E. to make something as great in amount, size, or importance as possible
6. accommodate	F. the amount of money you have available to spend
7. accessible	G. to provide with a place to live or to be stored in
8. emergency	H. a plan for how something will happen

II. Make the best choice to fill in the blanks with the given options in the box.

A. maximize your time spent at your destination
B. Particularly if you are going abroad, this may be a good idea in case in the case of an emergency
C. reserving lodging, deciding on meals and sightseeing
D. sometimes cheaper prices if you research your options carefully
E. making a calendar for your trip

Travel arrangements and an itinerary are two basic requirements for any trip. This has become a task that modern travelers must master. Making your own travel arrangements allows you flexibility and 1) _____ . In addition, designing an itinerary allows you to 2) _____ and make sure it fits into your schedule. Making travel arrangements includes choosing your destination, deciding on the method or transportation, 3) _____ .

Making an itinerary is much like 4) _____ . After making arrangements, you can choose how specific you want to be, leave room for error and share a copy of the itinerary with close family members or friends. 5) _____ .

Text B

Pre-reading Task: Answer the following questions before reading the text.

1. What's your opinions on business travel?

2. What suggestions or tips about travel can you find online?

3. What are other ways you can get suggestions about travelling?

Travel Tips for Elite Treatment

Want some tips on how the pros travel? Just ask a corporate travel manager. These are the people who spend billions on travel each year and help companies set policies that **dictate** how millions of people fly.[1] At the **annual** Global Business Travel Association(GBTA) **convention** in Boston last week, I gathered the best tips and **juiciest** secrets of corporate travel managers. Here are 7 ways to improve your travel:

1. Your company can earn frequent-flier points based on your travel.

Your company can get airline rewards for your frequent travel, based on the miles you fly or dollars spent. The program at United Airlines is called PerksPlus; American Airlines has Business Extra A, and Delta Air Lines has SkyBonus.[2] Some companies use the points for free trips for employees. Some travel managers use the points for a stash of **upgrades** they can give to their colleagues. Others use them to **defray** the cost of the travel department.

Big companies **negotiate discounts** with airlines, hotel chains and car-rental companies, which are **vying** to be **designated** "preferred providers" so they get the lion's share of bookings. To earn this designation, the providers often offer up corporate **perks**. "They get other benefits in addition to discounts," said Bob Smyth, a vice president at Gant Travel Management.

2. The cheapest times to buy vacation tickets are…

… the end of August/beginning of September and the end of December/beginning of January. At these times **consumers** are worn out on travel and bookings simply come to a **screeching** halt, says Jolee Goularte, travel manager at Align Technology Inc. In addition, corporate travel buying goes on **hiatus** in those two periods, especially between Christmas and New Year's.

3. It's worth joining every hotel **loyalty** program.

Just being a **run-of-the-mill** member can, **occasionally**, **qualify** you for room upgrades, late checkout times, access to **lounges** with snacks and drinks, free Wi-Fi, free breakfast and even **complimentary** laundry service—a shirt or two per day. Perks vary by hotel.[3]

Mary Motycka, travel manager at Alere Inc., in San Diego, went on vacation to Hawaii and signed up for the Hilton program a week before departure. She asked for an upgrade—and got it.

---

dictate v. 影响
annual adj. 一年的；一年一次的
convention n. 会议，大会
juicy adj. 生动有趣的；富于刺激性的

upgrade n. 升级；提高品级（或标准）
defray v. 支付
negotiate v. 谈判
discount n. 折扣
vie (with/for) v. 竞争
designate (as) v. 委任，指派
perk n. 额外津贴

consumer n. 消费者；消耗者
screech v. 尖叫；发出尖锐刺耳的声音
hiatus n. 裂缝；空隙

loyalty n. 忠诚
run-of-the-mill 一般化的；普通的
occasionally adv. 偶尔，间或
qualify v. 使具有资格，使合格
lounge n. （饭店，旅馆等的）休息室，会客厅
complimentary adj. 免费的

4. Load up your smartphone with emergency numbers and travel apps.

Having numbers in your phone for your car service (in case they don't show), for airport hotels near **hubs** (in case you miss a **connection** and get stranded) and for airlines can save time and save the day. Sometimes speed matters—you need to **grab** the last seat on a flight, or last room at a hotel.

Anna Mason of Maquet Cardiovascular of Wayne, N.J., notes her company makes employees pay for no-show charges at hotels, so having the phone number to **cancel** is **crucial**. "You should have it all in your phone, not on paper you're carrying around and won't find," she said.

Having the latest apps on your phone from airlines or the travel agencies you book with can get you the latest information on delays, gate changes, upgrades or lost-luggage tracking, said Richard Gomez, **associate** director at Procter & Gamble Co. in Cincinnati.

5. Be nice to the gate agent.

"They are really in control," said Judy Emma, corporate travel manager at Informatica in Redwood City, Calif.

Being nice to gate agents can be rewarded in improved seating or a boarding pass for an overbooked flight. As departure time nears for a flight, all control is turned over to gate agents. Calling your corporate travel manager or the airline reservation line can't help.

Companies can negotiate for the ability to put a number of employees into the gold, silver or **platinum** ranks at an airline, giving them access to priority **security**, boarding, seating and upgrades.[4] It works with hotels and car rental companies, too.

One **tactic** being used now: A company negotiates to have checked-baggage fees **waived**, with an airline simply **granting** bottom-level **elite** status to all company travelers.

6. Book inside your company's travel program.

A **survey** of travel managers indicated 22% of company travel, on average, gets booked outside the company program. That can mean travelers don't get discounts companies have negotiated, and companies don't get credit for trips with airlines, hotels and others. Also, if there is an emergency, your company may not know where to find you, and if there is a travel **disruption**, your corporate travel agent won't be able to rebook or **reroute** you.

7. Do pre-trip prep.

Travel managers suggest walking fire escape routes in

---

hub *n.* （兴趣、活动的）中心
connection *n.* 连接；联络
grab *v.* 攫取，抓取

cancel *v.* 取消，废除
crucial *adj.* 决定性的，重要的（+to/for）

associate *adj.* 副的

platinum *n.* 铂金
security *n.* 防备，防护
tactic *n.* 战术；策略
waive *v.* 放弃；撤回
grant *v.* 同意，准予
elite *adj.* 精英的

survey *n.* 调查；民意调查

disruption *n.* 妨碍；扰乱
reroute *v.* 给……重定路线，使改变路线

hotels so you'll know which way to go in an emergency. They encourage travelers to research destinations so you'll know how you're going to get from the airport to hotels, safe ways to move around.

"People walk through new cities with **blinders** on," said Pam McTeer, travel manager at First Data Corp. in Atlanta. She suggests making sure someone knows where you are at all times, even if it is just taking a taxi to a meeting. (837 words)

blinder *n.* （常用复数）马的眼罩

Notes

1. *These are the people who spend billions on travel each year and help companies set policies that dictate how millions of people fly.* 他们每年要花掉数以十亿计的差旅费，同时他们还帮助企业制定差旅政策，这些政策会对数百万人搭乘飞机的方式产生决定性影响。

    These 指代前一句里的 corporate travel manager。

2. *American Airlines has Business Extra A, and Delta Air Lines has SkyBonus.* 美国航空公司的计划名为 Business Extra A，达美航空公司则设置了 SkyBonus 计划。

3. *Just being a run-of-the-mill member can, occasionally, qualify you for room upgrades, late checkout times, access to lounges with snacks and drinks, free Wi-Fi, free breakfast and even complimentary laundry service—a shirt or two per day. Perks vary by hotel.* 只要成为普通会员，你就能偶尔享受到客房升级、延迟退房、获准进入提供点心和饮料的休息厅、免费无线上网、免费早餐甚至是附加的洗衣服务（每天一两件衬衫）。各酒店的优惠各有不同。

4. *Companies can negotiate for the ability to put a number of employees into the gold, silver or platinum ranks at an airline, giving them access to priority security, boarding, seating and upgrades.* 企业可和航空公司协商使一批员工成为金卡、银卡或铂金卡级别的会员，从而使他们可以优先安检、登机、就座和升级客舱。

Reading Comprehension

Decide whether the following statements are true (T) or false (F) according to the text.

( ) 1. Big companies negotiate discounts with airlines, hotel chains and car-rental companies, which are vying to be designated "preferred providers" so they get the lion's share of bookings.

( ) 2. It isn't worth joining every hotel loyalty program.

( ) 3. Having numbers in your phone for your car service (in case they don't show), for airport hotels near hubs and for airlines can save time and save the day.

( ) 4. Being nice to gate agents can be rewarded in improved seating or a boarding pass for an overbooked flight.

(   ) 5. A survey of travel managers indicated 50% of company travel, on average, gets booked outside the company program.

Vocabulary

Fill in the blanks with the given words or expressions. Change the form where necessary.

1. Therefore, Business and IT should form a _____ strategy together. (corporate)
2. The government has refused to _____ with the strikers. (negotiate)
3. So the issue is going to be which firm does all _____ go and buy their product from. (consumer)
4. This degree _____ you for teaching. (qualify)
5. The 7.10 train to London has been _____ . (cancel)
6. She broke into the conversation at a _____ moment. (crucial)
7. The series of _____ revealed that 39% of victims preferred not to talk about their problem. (survey)
8. The company has been _____ permission to build a shopping mall. (grant)

Section C / Extending Your English

I. Approaching the reading skill: scanning to locate specifically required information（查读）2

　　查读（scanning）的关键是带着问题去浏览。例如，打电话前从电话本上查号码，借书前从目录卡中找出索书号，旅游前从火车时刻表上找出所乘列车的车次和开车时间，从字典中查某个单词的词义，写文章时从某些资料中查找数据等。

　　查读时必须有具体、明确的要求，要有查找的目标；查读时尽快扫视所读材料，只有在找到所需信息时才仔细阅读该项内容；根据所需信息的性质集中注意与其有关的语言特点（如要找人物、地点就注意大写词，要找时间、数据就注意阿拉伯数字等）；一旦找到所需信息，达到目的，阅读便可终止，不必读完全文。

Practice: Scanning for information

　　Read the following flight schedule, then answer questions.

From: BEIJING, China (GMT+8)　　　　To: NEW YORK, United States (GMT-5)
PEK—Capital International Airport　　　EWR—Newark Liberty International Airport
　　　　　　　　　　　　　　　　　　JFK—John F. Kennedy International Airport
　　　　　　　　　　　　　　　　　　LGA—La Guardia Airport

DEPARTURE		ARRIVAL		FLIGHT INFORMATION		
Airport	Time	Airport	Time	Duration	Flight No	Equip
PEK	9:00a	JFK	9:30a	13h 30m	CA 0989	773
PEK	1:00p	JFK	1:30p	12h 30m	CA 0981	773
PEK	1:00p	JFK	1:30p	12h 30m	US 5351*	773
PEK	1:00p	JFK	1:30p	12h 30m	UA 7610*	773
PEK	5:00p	EWR	5:55p	12h 55m	CA 7213*	777
PEK	5:00p	EWR	5:55p	12h 55m	UA 0088	777

Questions:

1. If your boss wants to go to New York, which flight will arrive earliest?

2. If you take Flight UA0088, at which airport you will arrive?

3. Which flights will arrive at JFK at one o'clock in the afternoon?

4. When will the flights arrive at EWR?

5. Which flight takes the longest time to travel?

II. Applying the reading skill

Read the following passage and answer the questions after your reading.

Travel Arrangements

Travel arrangements can be **tricky** and **frustrating**, but if you follow some simple steps and keep some basic information in mind, you can take away those **hair-pulling** moments and make your vacation a memorable one.[1] Planning, research and following a simple plan can reward you with travel arrangements that will result in a near-perfect trip.

When making your travel arrangements, the first thing you need to do is confirm the events of your trip. If you are traveling simply to get away, you may want to make sure that the weather and general conditions will work for your trip. Maybe you are going for a specific event, such as a wedding or conference. Call ahead to confirm everything is going on as scheduled to avoid possible travel **conflicts**

---

tricky *adj.* 微妙的；难处理的
frustrate *v.* 挫败；阻挠；使感到灰心
hair-pulling *adj.* 令人挠头的

conflict *n.* 冲突，分歧

before you go to avoid incurring cancellation fees.

Your next step is booking your flight. Flights are normally less expensive when booking at least three weeks in advance. Research the major airlines and **charter** flights to find the best deals. Remember, after booking, if you use a major airline, you have 24 hours to change or cancel your flight.

When you get your flights arranged or if you use other transportation, your next step will be to get a reservation for your hotel or lodging **accommodations**. If you are interested in a hotel, you can use a travel website to find out the general **rates** and book there, but first you may want to check directly with hotel websites. Sometimes booking directly can save money on hotels, but travel websites also may offer **coupons** or discounts.

Other types of accommodations include **campsites**, bed-and-breakfasts or home trading. Camping and bed-and-breakfasts have specific websites, which may require calling in your reservations. Use Google to search for accommodations in the area you are traveling, and visit the website of the one you choose for booking information.

Home **exchanging** is a new way to stay in a different city and can save money, as you **swap** your home with another person.

Whether you decide to rent a car or use public transportation, you will need to know your options and what you decide in advance. Some cities see a **shortage** of rental cars, so booking in advance is essential.

If you decide on public transportation, you will want to research taxicab rates **versus** shuttles in the area and make a decision on what is right for you. Keep in mind, shuttles generally take longer to reach their destinations, although they may provide less expensive transportation.

Finally, you will want to make sure that you have researched all of the things that you plan to do and the sites you plan to see. Be sure to schedule your plans so that you leave time to enjoy the **attractions** you visit. If it all seems a bit **overwhelming** to you, travel agents are available to provide you with direction and **assistance**. (484 words)

---

charter *n.* （船只、巴士、飞机等的）租赁，包租

accommodation *n.* 住处；膳宿
rate *n.* 比例，比率

coupon *n.* 赠券；减价优待券
campsite *n.* 露营地

exchange *v.* 交换；调换
swap *v.* 交换

shortage *n.* 缺少，匮乏

versus *prep.* 与……相对

attraction *n.* 吸引物；喜闻乐见的事物
overwhelming *adj.* 压倒的；势不可挡的
assistance *n.* 援助，帮助

Notes

1. Travel arrangements can be tricky and frustrating, but if you follow some simple steps and keep some basic information in mind, you can take away those hair-pulling moments and make your

vacation a memorable one. 旅行安排很令人沮丧，但是，如果你能遵循一些简单的步骤并牢记一些简单的信息，就会避免那些令人挠头的时刻，拥有一个难忘的旅行。

Exercise: Answer the following questions according to the text.

1. What will result in a near-perfect trip?

2. How many steps are there when you make your travel arrangements?

Section D / Self-evaluation

After learning this unit, I have grasped

Items	100%	80%	60%	Below 50%
Words				
Grammar				
Reading				

Notes to this unit:

New Words and Expressions

A

a series of		一系列	R-1-6-A
a variety of		各种各样的	R-1-2-B
absolutely	adv.	绝对地，完全地	R-1-3-C
access	n.	（使用某物或接近某人的）机会	R-1-6-C
accessible	adj.	可（或易）接近的；可（或易）进入的	R-1-8-A
accessory	n.	配件；（女用手提包等）的装饰品	R-1-3-A
accommodation	n.	住处；膳宿	R-1-8-C
accomplish	v.	完成；达到（目的）	R-1-1-C
accomplishment	n.	成就，成绩	R-1-4-A
accounting	n.	会计	R-1-2-A
acknowledge	v.	承认	R-1-3-B
acquaintance	n.	相识的人，熟人	R-1-1-A
adapt	v.	使适应	R-1-2-B
adequately	adv.	足够地，充分地	R-1-2-A
adult	n.	成年人	R-1-1-B
agenda	n.	议程	R-1-6-A
ahead of		在……之前	R-1-1-C
aid	v.	帮助，援助	R-1-2-C
alarm	n.	闹钟	R-1-3-A
allocate	v.	分配，分派	R-1-6-A
allot	v.	分配；分配给	R-1-7-C
along with		与……在一起	R-1-6-A
alternate	adj.	供选择的；供替换的	R-1-8-A
alternative	n.	选择；供选择的东西	R-1-4-B
alternatively	adv.	二者择一地	R-1-6-B
alumnus	n.	校友	R-1-2-A
ambition	n.	雄心，抱负	R-1-1-A
amount	n.	量，数量，数额；总数	R-1-5-A
analyst	n.	分析师	R-1-4-C
announcement	n.	公告	R-1-6-C
annual	adj.	一年的；一年一次的	R-1-8-B
apparent	adj.	明显的，清楚的	R-1-1-B
applause	n.	鼓掌欢迎；喝彩	R-1-7-C
applicant	n.	申请人，求职者	R-1-2-B

apply to		适用于；运用	R-1-1-B
appreciation	n.	欣赏，鉴赏；赏识	R-1-7-B
appropriate	adj.	适当的，恰当的	R-1-5-B
approximate	adj.	大约的，大概的	R-1-8-A
armor	n.	盔甲	R-1-1-B
arouse	v.	唤起；激动；使奋发	R-1-7-C
arrange	v.	安排，整理	R-1-5-A
as a result		结果	R-1-6-B
aspect	n.	方面	R-1-4-B
assess	v.	评估	R-1-3-B
assimilate	v.	理解；吸收	R-1-4-A
assistance	n.	援助，帮助	R-1-8-C
associate	adj.	副的	R-1-8-B
at ease		不拘束，自在	R-1-3-C
at intervals		不时；到处	R-1-5-C
atmosphere	n.	气氛	R-1-6-C
attachment	n.	附件	R-1-6-A
attendance	n.	到场；出席	R-1-7-B
attendee	n	出席者；在场者	R-1-6-A
attire	n.	衣服，服装	R-1-2-C
attraction	n.	吸引物；喜闻乐见的事物	R-1-8-C
attribute	v.	归于，属于	R-1-4-A
audience	n.	听众，观众	R-1-1-A
availability	n.	可得到的东西（或人）	R-1-8-A
available	adj.	可用的，在手边的；可利用的	R-1-7-B
avoid	v.	避开，躲开	R-1-1-B
aware	adj.	知道的；意识到的	R-1-3-B
awesome	adj.	极好的	R-1-2-A

B

back and forth		来回地，往复地	R-1-5-A
back off		后退；让步	R-1-3-A
background	n.	背景	R-1-2-A
balance	n.	平衡，均衡	R-1-2-B
barrier	n.	障碍	R-1-4-B
base on		使建立在……基础上	R-1-1-A
baseball	n.	棒球	R-1-1-B
baseline	n.	（用于比较的）基础；起点	R-1-1-A
be responsible for		对……有责任	R-1-6-A

be toast		（非正式）完蛋了，倒霉了	R-1-3-B
bear in mind		牢记	R-1-1-C
beforehand	adv.	提前，预先	R-1-2-B
beneficial	adj.	有益的；有利的	R-1-1-B
blinder	n.	马的眼罩	R-1-8-B
boastful	adj.	自夸的；爱自夸的	R-1-1-A
bother	v.	烦扰	R-1-5-B
break the ice		打破沉默	R-1-3-A
briefing	n.	简报	R-1-4-A
bring up		提出；养育	R-1-3-B
brush up on		复习，重温	R-1-2-B
budget	n.	预算；预算费；生活费，经费	R-1-8-A
burn up		消耗；烧毁	R-1-5-B
butt	n.	（口语）屁股	R-1-3-C

C

calculate	v.	计划；打算；把……考虑进去	R-1-8-A
campsite	n.	露营地	R-1-8-C
cancel	v.	取消，废除	R-1-8-B
capability	n.	能力	R-1-6-B
career	n.	职业；事业	R-1-1-C
casually	adv.	随意地，休闲地	R-1-2-B
celebrate	v.	庆祝	R-1-7-C
cement	v.	接合，巩固	R-1-4-A
certification	n.	证明，保证	R-1-4-A
challenge	v.	质疑；挑战	R-1-1-C
chancellor	n.	（某些美国大学的）校长	R-1-3-A
charge into		冲进	R-1-3-B
charter	n.	（船只、巴士、飞机等的）租赁，包租	R-1-8-C
cheat sheet		小抄，备忘单	R-1-2-A
chronological	adj.	按时间的前后顺序排列的	R-1-6-B
circumstance	n.	状况	R-1-4-B
claim	v.	声称；断言	R-1-1-C
clarification	n.	澄清，说明	R-1-5-C
coach	n.	教练	R-1-1-B
collaboration	n.	合作	R-1-6-B
collection	n.	成堆物品	R-1-6-C
column	n.	列，栏	R-1-6-A
combination	n.	结合，联合	R-1-6-A

committed	adj.	忠诚的；坚定的	R-1-3-A
communicate	v.	沟通，交流	R-1-1-B
competitor	n.	竞争者，对手	R-1-2-C
complex	adj.	复杂的	R-1-5-B
complimentary	adj.	免费的	R-1-8-B
composition	n.	构成；构图；成分	R-1-1-A
conclusion	n.	结论，结尾	R-1-6-A
conference	n.	讨论（会），会议	R-1-6-B
confident	adj.	自信的	R-1-1-A
confirm	v.	证实；确定	R-1-7-B
conflict	n.	冲突，分歧	R-1-8-C
confusing	adj.	令人困惑的	R-1-1-B
connection	n.	连接；联络	R-1-8-B
consideration	n.	体谅；考虑	R-1-4-A
consist of		由……组成	R-1-2-B
constant	adj.	始终如一的；坚定的；忠实的	R-1-1-A
consumer	n.	消费者；消耗者	R-1-8-B
contact	n.	交往；联系，联络	R-1-1-A
contribute to		有助于；促成	R-1-6-A
convention	n.	会议，大会	R-1-8-B
convey	v.	表达，传达	R-1-2-B
cosmopolitan	adj.	世界性的，国际性的	R-1-8-A
costly	adj.	昂贵的，费用大的	R-1-4-A
coupon	n.	赠券；减价优待券	R-1-8-C
critical	adj.	紧要的，关键性的；危急的	R-1-1-A
criticize	v.	批评；评论	R-1-3-B
cross one's finger		两指交叉以求好运	R-1-3-C
crucial	adj.	决定性的，重要的	R-1-8-B
cubicle	n.	（大房间中隔出的）小室	R-1-4-B
current	adj.	当前的，流行的	R-1-5-B
cut down		削减，缩短	R-1-5-B

D

database	n.	资料库；数据库	R-1-5-A
decrease	v.	减少，减小	R-1-5-B
define	v.	使明确，规定	R-1-6-A
definitely	adv.	明确地；肯定地	R-1-1-B
defray	v.	支付	R-1-8-B
demonstrate	v.	展示，说明	R-1-4-A

departure	n.	离开；出发，起程	R-1-8-A
depend on		依靠；信赖	R-1-1-A
designate (as)	v.	委任，指派	R-1-8-B
designation	n.	任命；委派	R-1-6-A
detail	n.	细节，详情	R-1-2-C
dictate	v.	影响	R-1-8-B
disaster	n.	灾难，不幸	R-1-2-C
discount	n.	折扣	R-1-8-B
discourage	v.	设法阻止（某事物）	R-1-6-C
disruption	n.	妨碍；扰乱	R-1-8-B
disseminate	v.	散播；宣传	R-1-7-A
distract	v.	使某人分心	R-1-6-B
distress	v.	使苦恼，使忧伤	R-1-1-B
distribute	v.	分发	R-1-6-A
document	n.	文件	R-1-6-B
documentation	n.	文件	R-1-6-C
double-check	v.	将……仔细检查；复核	R-1-5-B
drag into		硬把……拉扯进	R-1-3-B

E

eat away		侵蚀；蚕食	R-1-4-A
eat up		消耗，吃完	R-1-5-B
(be) eager to		热切的	R-1-6-C
economist	n.	经济学家	R-1-4-C
edge	n.	优势	R-1-1-A
ego	n.	自我；自负	R-1-1-C
elaborate	v.	详细制定；详尽阐述	R-1-1-A
eliminate	v.	去除，排除	R-1-4-A
elite	adj.	精英的	R-1-8-B
elsewhere	adv.	在别处	R-1-4-C
embarrass	v.	使窘迫；使不好意思，使局促不安	R-1-1-A
emerge	v.	浮现	R-1-4-C
emergency	n.	紧急情况；突发事件；非常时刻	R-1-8-A
encounter	v.	遇见	R-1-4-B
ensure	v.	保证；担保	R-1-1-A
enthusiasm	n.	热情	R-1-3-B
entry-level	adj.	入门级的	R-1-4-A
equitable	adj.	公平的，公正的	R-1-4-B
error	n.	错误，差错	R-1-8-A

error	n.	错误，差错	R-1-8-A
estimate	n.	估价；评价	R-1-5-A
etiquette	n.	礼节；礼仪	R-1-1-A
Eve	n.	前一天，前夕	R-1-1-B
exceed	v.	超过；超出	R-1-7-A
exchange	v.	交换；调换	R-1-8-C
exclude	v.	排除	R-1-4-B
exhibit	v.	展现	R-1-4-B
expectation	n.	预料；期望	R-1-3-A
expire	v.	期满，终止	R-1-4-C
extend	v.	延长，延伸；伸出	R-1-1-B
external	adj.	外面的	R-1-6-C
extra	adj.	额外的；外加的	R-1-1-B
eye contact		眼神交流	R-1-1-B
eye to eye		眼对眼的	R-1-1-A

F

face-to-face	adj.	当面的	R-1-6-B
facilitate	v.	促进；帮助	R-1-7-A
facilitator	n.	促进者	R-1-6-A
factor	n.	因素；要素	R-1-7-B
fade	v.	凋谢；消失	R-1-4-C
familiarize	v.	使某人/自己熟悉某事物	R-1-6-B
fancy	adj.	色彩鲜艳的，复杂的	R-1-6-B
fashion	n.	时装，时尚	R-1-2-C
figure out		理解；想出	R-1-4-B
fill up		装满，填满	R-1-5-A
fiscal	adj.	财政的；会计的	R-1-4-B
flexible	adj.	可弯曲的，易弯曲的；柔韧的；有弹性的	R-1-8-A
flip	v.	急促转动，蹦跳	R-1-5-A
follow-up	n.	后续行动	R-1-4-A
fondly	adv.	深情地	R-1-1-B
font	n.	字体	R-1-6-B
for instance		例如，譬如	R-1-1-B
format	n.	（某事物的）总体安排，计划	R-1-6-B
former	adj.	前者的；以前的	R-1-3-A
formulate	v.	制定	R-1-6-C
forthright	adj.	直率的；坦白的	R-1-3-B
foundation	n.	（作为某事的）基本原则，思想或事实；基础	R-1-6-A
frustrate	v.	挫败；阻挠；使感到灰心	R-1-8-C

G

gastronomy	n.	美食法	R-1-8-A
gender-neutral	adj.	中性的	R-1-1-C
gesture	n.	姿势；手势	R-1-1-A
get along		进展	R-1-3-C
get in the habit of		养成习惯	R-1-5-B
go over		察看	R-1-5-B
go through		通过，经历	R-1-5-B
goal	n.	目标，目的	R-1-1-C
gossip	n.	流言蜚语；闲话	R-1-3-B
grab	v.	攫取，抓取	R-1-8-B
gracious	adj.	亲切的；仁慈的	R-1-3-B
grant	v.	同意，准予	R-1-8-B
guarantee	v.	保障；保证……免受损失	R-1-1-A

H

hair-pulling	adj.	令人挠头的	R-1-8-C
hairstylist	n.	发型设计师	R-1-3-B
handle	v.	对待，处理	R-1-1-B
handout	n.	讲课提纲；讲义	R-1-7-B
hang back		却步，犹豫	R-1-4-B
harassment	n.	烦恼；骚扰	R-1-4-A
headset	n.	头戴式受话器；双耳式耳机	R-1-6-B
hesitant	adj.	犹豫的	R-1-6-C
hiatus	n.	裂缝；空隙	R-1-8-B
high-end	adj.	高端的	R-1-4-C
highlight	n.	最突出（或最精彩）的部分；最重要（或最有趣）的事情	R-1-7-B
hinder	v.	阻碍，妨碍	R-1-5-C
host	n.	主持人	R-1-7-B
hub	n.	（兴趣、活动的）中心	R-1-8-B
hyperlink	n.	超链接	R-1-6-B

I

icebreaker	n.	打破僵局的话语或行为；破冰船	R-1-1-A
ideal	adj.	理想的，最合适的	R-1-6-C
identify	v.	识别，鉴定	R-1-4-B
illegal	adj.	违法的	R-1-4-B
impact	n.	影响；作用	R-1-1-A
impression	n.	印象	R-1-1-A

impulse	n.	冲动	R-1-4-B
in addition		另外；此外；加之	R-1-1-A
in advance of		在……的前面	R-1-6-A
in a hurry		匆忙	R-1-4-B
in all shapes and sizes		以各种形式，各式各样	R-1-2-B
in case		倘若，如果	R-1-6-A
in combination with		与……结合（联合）	R-1-6-A
in relation to		有关	R-1-4-A
in someone/something's favor		对某人/某事有利	R-1-6-B
in short supply		供不应求	R-1-4-C
in terms of		就……而论；在……方面	R-1-5-B
in the same light		相同地	R-1-6-B
inbound	adj.	（电话）打进来的，呼入的	R-1-5-B
incompetent	adj.	不能胜任的	R-1-3-C
independent	adj.	独立的，自治的	R-1-1-B
indicate	v.	指示；表明	R-1-3-B
indirectly	adv.	间接地	R-1-3-B
indulge	v.	使自己高兴一下；让自己享受一下	R-1-8-A
informal	adj.	非正式的	R-1-6-B
inject	v.	引入；投入	R-1-7-C
input	n.	意见	R-1-6-C
insert	v.	插（话等），插入	R-1-5-B
insight	n.	洞察力，眼光	R-1-1-A
instead of		代替	R-1-5-A
instill	v.	灌输	R-1-4-A
institution	n.	机构	R-1-6-C
interact	v.	互动	R-1-1-A
interfere	v.	干涉；妨碍	R-1-3-A
intern	n.	实习生	R-1-3-C
internship	n.	实习，实习岗位	R-1-2-A
involve	v.	使卷入，连累；牵涉	R-1-1-A
issue	n.	事情；问题	R-1-3-B
item	n.	项目，条款	R-1-6-A
itinerary	n.	旅程；路线；行程安排	R-1-8-A

J

jot	v.	草草记下	R-1-5-A
juicy	adj.	生动有趣的；富于刺激性的	R-1-8-B

K

keynote speaker	n.	主讲人，主题发言人	R-1-7-B

L

lack	v.	缺少，缺乏	R-1-1-B
lay out		设计；安排；陈列	R-1-3-A
leadership	n.	领导能力	R-1-2-B
lean	v.	（使）倾斜，屈身	R-1-1-A
legend	n.	传说，传奇	R-1-4-A
link	n.	链接	R-1-6-B
local	adj.	当地的，本地的	R-1-2-A
location	n.	位置；场所	R-1-5-B
logistics	n.	物流；后勤；组织工作	R-1-6-A
longstanding	adj.	长期存在的	R-1-1-C
loose	adj.	不严密的，不确切的，不明确的	R-1-8-A
lounge	n.	（饭店，旅馆等的）休息室，会客厅	R-1-8-B
loyalty	n.	忠诚	R-1-8-B

M

maintain	v.	维持；保持	R-1-7-B
make sense		有意义	R-1-4-C
make-your-own	adj.	自制的	R-1-7-C
mandate	v.	命令，要求	R-1-4-A
manner	n.	礼貌；规矩	R-1-1-A
manufacture	v.	制造，加工	R-1-4-A
master	v.	精通，掌握	R-1-1-B
meaningless	adj.	无意义的；无目的的	R-1-5-B
measure	v.	测量；估量	R-1-4-B
medieval	adj.	中世纪的	R-1-1-B
men-dominated	adj.	男性占首要地位的	R-1-1-C
mentor	v.	为……出谋划策；指导	R-1-4-A
metaphor	n.	暗喻；比喻	R-1-2-A
minimum	n.	最低限度，最小量	R-1-5-B
minutes	n.	会议记录	R-1-6-A
mission	n.	使命，天职	R-1-2-A
moderate	adj.	（通常指政治方面）不极端的，温和的	R-1-4-C
moderator	n.	会议主席，仲裁者	R-1-6-C
modest	adj.	适度的；中等的	R-1-4-C
moreover	adv.	并且，此外	R-1-5-A
multi-tasking	adj.	同时处理多重任务的	R-1-5-A

mutual	adj.	相互的；共同的	R-1-2-B

N

negative	adj.	否定的，负面的	R-1-2-B
negotiate	v.	谈判	R-1-8-B
networking	n.	人际关系网	R-1-1-C
nonprofit	adj.	非营利的	R-1-6-C
notepad	n.	笔记本，记事手册	R-1-2-C
not-for-profit organization		非营利性机构	R-1-2-A
nuisance	n.	讨厌的人；讨厌的东西	R-1-3-A

O

objective	n.	目标；目的	R-1-6-A
obtain	v.	取得某物	R-1-5-C
occasionally	adv.	偶尔，间或	R-1-8-B
on equal ground		平等地	R-1-1-A
on the spot		立刻；当场	R-1-5-A
ongoing	adj.	前进的，进行的	R-1-4-A
opportunity	n.	机会，时机	R-1-2-A
option	n.	选择	R-1-5-B
orientation	n.	定方位，方向，倾向	R-1-4-A
outcome	n.	结果；结局	R-1-6-A
outdated	adj.	过时的，旧式的	R-1-1-C
outgoing	adj.	向外的	R-1-5-A
outline	n.	要点；大纲	R-1-6-C
outspoken	adj.	直言的；坦率的	R-1-6-C
overcome	v.	战胜，克服	R-1-4-B
overlook	v.	看漏；忽略	R-1-7-B
over-the-top	adj.	夸大其词的，过分的	R-1-6-B
overwhelming	adj.	压倒的；势不可挡的	R-1-8-C

P

pace	n.	速度，步调	R-1-4-C
packaging	n.	包装	R-1-3-C
pad	n.	便条纸簿	R-1-5-B
palm	n.	手掌	R-1-1-A
panel	n.	专门小组	R-1-2-B
paperwork	n.	表格；文件，资料	R-1-3-A

paraphrase	v.	将……释义	R-1-5-B
participant	n.	参与者	R-1-6-A
participate	v.	参加；参与	R-1-7-C
pass on		传递	R-1-4-A
password	n.	口令；密码	R-1-3-A
peer	n.	同龄人；社会地位相同的人	R-1-7-B
perk	n.	额外津贴	R-1-8-B
perplexed	a.	困惑的；不知所措的	R-1-3-B
personal	adj.	个人的	R-1-1-A
personnel	n.	职员	R-1-5-C
perspective	n.	看法	R-1-6-C
philosophy	n.	哲学	R-1-4-A
pick up		接电话；拾起	R-1-5-B
pitch in		使劲地干起来	R-1-6-B
platinum	n.	铂金	R-1-8-B
policy	n.	政策，方针	R-1-5-C
polish	v.	修正，改进	R-1-2-B
portion	n.	（一）部分	R-1-7-C
potential	n.	潜力，潜能	R-1-2-B
pound	v.	剧烈跳动	R-1-3-C
practical	adj.	实际的；实用的	R-1-1-A
precise	adj.	精确的，准确的	R-1-2-A
predict	v.	预测，预言	R-1-2-B
preference	n.	偏爱；偏爱的人或事物	R-1-8-A
preparation	n.	准备	R-1-2-A
presentation	n.	陈述	R-1-6-B
presenter	n.	出席者，提出者	R-1-6-A
presume	v.	冒昧地做某事；越权做某事	R-1-3-B
prevailing	adj.	盛行的；主流的	R-1-3-B
previous	adj.	（时间或顺序上）在先的；先前的	R-1-6-C
primary	adj.	首要的，主要的	R-1-1-C
prime	adj.	最好的；主要的	R-1-5-A
principle	n.	原则；原理	R-1-1-B
prior	adj.	在先的	R-1-6-A
prioritize	v.	把事情按优先顺序排好；优先处理；使优先	R-1-5-B
proactive	adj.	有前瞻性的；积极主动的	R-1-4-A
procedure	n.	步骤，手续	R-1-5-C
processor	n.	（计算机）中央处理器	R-1-6-B
productivity	n.	生产率，生产力	R-1-5-A

professional	n.	专业人士	R-1-1-C
	adj.	职业的，专业的	R-1-2-A
profusely	adv.	丰富地；大量地	R-1-3-A
pronunciate	v.	发音，读法	R-1-1-B
prophet	n.	预言者，先知	R-1-4-C
proverb	n.	谚语，格言	R-1-2-A
pull away		拉掉，扯掉	R-1-5-B
pursue	v.	继续进行	R-1-3-C
pushy	adj.	有进取心的	R-1-2-B
put back		把……放回原处；拖延	R-1-5-B
put together		拼，组成整体	R-1-6-B

Q

qualification	n.	资格，职权；能力	R-1-1-A
qualify	v.	使具有资格，使合格	R-1-8-B
quit	v.	离开；辞职	R-1-3-A
quote	n.	引语，引文	R-1-1-A

R

rate	n.	比例，比率	R-1-8-C
rather than		而不是	R-1-5-B
realm	n.	（活动或兴趣的）领域	R-1-6-C
reasonable	adj.	合理的	R-1-3-B
recall	v.	回想，回忆	R-1-1-B
recap	v.	简要地复述	R-1-6-C
receptionist	n.	前台接待员	R-1-5-B
recipient	n.	接受者；收件人	R-1-5-A
recommend	v.	推荐；建议	R-1-3-A
referrer	n.	推荐人；介绍人	R-1-2-A
refresher	n.	补习课程	R-1-4-A
regardless of		不管，不顾	R-1-2-B
register	v.	登记，注册	R-1-6-B
related to		与……有关	R-1-7-A
relationship	n.	关系	R-1-1-B
relevant	adj.	有关的，切题的	R-1-6-B
rely on		依赖，依靠	R-1-8-A
render	v.	给予，提供	R-1-1-B
replay	v.	重放；重播	R-1-5-A
represent	v.	表示，代表	R-1-6-A

representative	n.	代表	R-1-2-B
reputation	n.	声誉,名声	R-1-3-B
requirement	n.	需要；必需品,要求；必要条件；规定	R-1-8-A
reroute	v.	给……重定路线,使改变路线	R-1-8-B
reservation	n.	预订	R-1-8-A
reserved	adj.	内向的,矜持的	R-1-2-B
resist	v.	忍耐,忍住	R-1-4-B
response	n.	回答；反应	R-1-1-B
restatement	n.	重申	R-1-6-A
résumé	n.	〈美〉履历,简历	R-1-2-A
revise	v.	修改,修正	R-1-7-A
run-of-the-mill	adj.	一般化的；普通的	R-1-8-B

S

sales-oriented	adj.	销售型的,以销售为导向的	R-1-5-C
schedule	v.	把……安排在；排定；预定	R-1-5-A
screech	v.	尖叫；发出尖锐刺耳的声音	R-1-8-B
script	n.	（演讲,戏剧,广播等的）脚本,底稿	R-1-5-B
sector	n.	部分；部门	R-1-1-B
security	n.	防备,防护	R-1-8-B
seminar	n.	专题讨论会	R-1-7-B
series	n.	一系列的事物	R-1-6-A
session	n.	（进行某活动连续的）一段时间	R-1-6-B
set foot		踏上；涉足	R-1-3-C
set up		建立,建造	R-1-5-B
severe	adj.	严厉的,剧烈的	R-1-4-C
shelf life		货架期,保质期	R-1-4-C
shortage	n.	缺少,匮乏	R-1-8-C
shrewd	adj.	精明的；敏锐的	R-1-4-C
sign	v.	签（名）	R-1-1-B
significant	adj.	重要的,有含义的	R-1-4-B
similarity	n.	相似点,相似之处	R-1-2-B
simmer	v.	即将爆发；内心充满	R-1-3-B
simply	adv.	仅仅	R-1-3-A
slogan	n.	标语,口号	R-1-4-A
snack	n.	小吃,点心	R-1-7-C
social responsibility		社会责任	R-1-2-A
software	n.	软件	R-1-2-B
sole	n.	单独的；唯一的	R-1-1-A

solve	v.	解决，解答	R-1-2-B
speakerphone	n.	无绳电话，免提电话	R-1-5-A
specific	adj.	特殊的，特定的	R-1-7-A
staff	n.	（全体）职员；（全体）工作人员	R-1-7-A
stage	n.	舞台	R-1-1-A
stakeholder	n.	参与者；相关人员；利益共享者	R-1-7-A
start off		开始	R-1-3-C
status	n.	情形；状况；情势	R-1-7-A
stick to		忠于，信守	R-1-5-A
storm into		冲进	R-1-3-B
straightforward	adj.	简单的；易懂的	R-1-1-B
strategy	n.	策略	R-1-3-C
strength	n.	长处	R-1-3-B
strike up		开始（交谈），建立起（友谊等）	R-1-1-B
substantial	adj.	数目大的；可观的	R-1-4-A
subtle	adj.	微妙的；隐约的	R-1-4-B
success	n.	成功	R-1-1-A
successful	adj.	成功的	R-1-2-A
summarize	v.	总结	R-1-5-B
sundae	n.	圣代冰淇淋	R-1-7-C
supervisor	n.	监督人，管理人	R-1-3-C
(be) sure to do		必定（做）	R-1-7-A
survey	n.	调查；民意调查	R-1-8-B
swap	v.	交换	R-1-8-C
sweat	v.	出汗	R-1-1-A
symposium	n.	讨论会；座谈会	R-1-7-B
system	n.	系统	R-1-6-B

T

tactic	n.	战术；策略	R-1-8-B
take ... seriously		认真对待……	R-1-2-A
take charge of		开始管理，接管	R-1-5-C
take credit		居功	R-1-4-B
take into account		考虑到；体谅	R-1-8-A
take note of		注意	R-1-7-A
take over		接收；接管	R-1-3-B
take up		占用	R-1-5-B
target	n.	目标	R-1-7-B
technically	adv.	技术上	R-1-1-C

New Words and Expressions

technology	n.	技术，工艺	R-1-5-B
tend to		有……的倾向	R-1-5-C
terrifying	adj.	恐怖的	R-1-3-C
thoughtful	adj.	深思熟虑的	R-1-6-C
threat	n.	威胁	R-1-2-A
time-consuming	adj.	费时的	R-1-5-B
tone	n.	某事物的格调或特性	R-1-6-B
topic	n.	话题	R-1-6-A
tout	v.	兜售，推销（商品或服务）；拉生意	R-1-4-A
traditional	adj.	传统的；惯例的	R-1-7-B
transportation	n.	运输工具；交通车辆	R-1-8-A
trap	n.	陷阱；圈套	R-1-4-C
tricky	adj.	微妙的；难处理的	R-1-8-C
trustworthy	adj.	值得信赖的，可靠的	R-1-1-B
tuition	n.	学费	R-1-4-C
turnover	n.	（人员的）流动率	R-1-4-A
tutu	n.	芭蕾舞短裙	R-1-3-B

U

undergraduate	n.	大学生	R-1-3-C
unethical	adj.	不道德的	R-1-4-B
uninterrupted	adj.	不间断的，连续的	R-1-5-B
upgrade	n.	升级；提高品级（或标准）	R-1-8-B
upload	v.	上传	R-1-6-B
unrelated	adj.	不相关的	R-1-3-B

V

validate	v.	使有效，确认	R-1-4-A
valuable	adj.	贵重的，宝贵的；有价值的	R-1-1-C
vary	v.	改变	R-1-5-C
versus	prep.	与……相对	R-1-8-C
video conferencing		视频会议，电视会议	R-1-2-B
vie (with / for)	v.	竞争	R-1-8-B
vital	adj.	极其重要的，必不可少的	R-1-7-A

W

wage	n.	薪水；工资	R-1-4-C
waive	v.	放弃；撤回	R-1-8-B
wander	v.	离题；闲逛	R-1-5-B

webcam	n.	网络摄像头	R-1-6-B
weigh in		参与；发表评论	R-1-3-B
what's more		而且，此外	R-1-6-B
wheelchair	n.	轮椅	R-1-1-B
wince	v.	畏缩；退避	R-1-1-B
with flying colors		出色地	R-1-3-A
without hesitation		毫不犹豫地，不假思索地	R-1-2-A
workplace	n.	工作场所	R-1-3-A
workspace	n.	工作空间	R-1-6-B
wrestle	v.	斗争	R-1-4-C

Y

yell	v.	大叫；叫着说	R-1-4-B